MW01127118

CONTROL
IN BUSINESS
ORGANIZATIONS

LT 30

CONTROL
IN BUSINESS
ORGANIZATIONS

Kenneth A. Merchant
Harvard Graduate School of Business

BALLINGER PUBLISHING COMPANY
Cambridge, Massachusetts
A Subsidiary of Harper & Row, Publishers, Inc.

© 1985 Kenneth A. Merchant

All rights reserved. No part of this publication may be reproduced, stored in a retrieval system, or transmitted in any form or by any means, electronic, mechanical, photocopying, recording and/or otherwise without the prior written permission of the publishers.

Library of Congress Cataloging in Publication Data

Merchant, Kenneth A.
  Control in business organizations.

  Bibliography: p. 139
  Includes index.
  1. Controllership. I. Title.
HG4026.M47 1984   658.1′51   84-11374
ISBN 0-88730-161-4 (previously published by
  Pitman Publishing Inc., ISBN 0-273-01914-7)

Manufactured in the United States of America

CONTENTS

FOREWORD

The task of influencing the behavior of people to achieve organizational objectives has always been recognized to be of considerable importance. In their desire to gain control over the behavior of people, business organizations use a variety of mechanisms, including personal supervision, job descriptions, rules, standard operation procedures, performance appraisal, budgets, standard costing, accounting-information, and incentive compensation systems. Taken together, these mechanisms comprise the "organizational control system."

In recognition of the critical importance of control in organizations, the literature on this subject (managerial as well as academic) has grown voluminous. A variety of different approaches or schools of organizational control have appeared based upon the differing perspectives of sociologists, administrative theorists, psychologists, and operations researchers. These divergent approaches have led to a significant body of concepts and insights concerning control, but not to a well developed or integrated theory of organizational control. The literature contains many different definitions of control. The concepts of control range from "choosing operating and enforcement rules" to "interpersonal influence activities;" from "keeping things on track" to "increasing the probability that people will behave in ways that lead to the achievement of organizational objectives." As a result, the body of knowledge of organizational control currently has a fragmented quality. This is simply a characteristic that is typical of scientific fields during their early stages of evolution, and thus there is a need for some integrative work to bring order to this field.

Control In Business Organizations by Kenneth Merchant is directed toward satisfying this need for an integration of control theory. The book takes a managerial perspective of control in business organizations. It uses the concept of "the object of control" as the guiding organizing principle to tie together many of the divergent control concepts and insights developed in the field. Controls are analyzed in terms of whether the focus of control is on results, actions, or personnel.

The framework used by Merchant in this book proves to be a useful organizing scheme to help integrate a great many of the "bits and pieces" of control concepts, research findings, and ideas. He sees the function of control as helping to ensure the proper behaviors of people in organizations. This broad concept of the ultimate aim of control is, in my judgment, more useful than narrower conceptualizations of control as a set of devices such as rules, procedures, measurement, and rewards. Such things are the tools of control and not control per se.

The book also makes a contribution by focusing attention on a variety of important issues of control systems design: How to make controls tighter or looser, and understanding the negative side effects which are either inherent in control systems or by-products of systems that have been poorly designed. It also contributes to an action orientation by highlighting the decisions which must be made in the design of a control system: the choice of controls used (results, actions, or personnel), tight versus loose controls, and the use of multiple controls.

Although the topic of control has received a great deal of recent attention, the field is still in its relative infancy. It is a significant and fertile area for academic inquiry as well as managerial innovation. This book makes a significant contribution by helping to enlarge our general understanding of organizational control as well as our ability to apply concepts and ideas of control to actual practice.

Eric G. Flamholtz

PREFACE

The motivation for this book was derived from the confusion and frustration I felt as I tried to develop and teach an elective course in management control for the second-year MBA curriculum at the Harvard Business School. I was familiar with the topics that were typically included in management control courses, such as planning and budgeting systems, responsibility centers, cost allocations, transfer prices, and variance analyses. But I also felt that students needed to be made aware of other control-related topics, such as internal controls, internal audits, and policies and procedures that were normally not included. This led me to do some thinking about the desirable state of "good control" in an organization and how these various tools and mechanisms contribute toward its realization. The result was a new, broader control framework which is described in this book.

As I describe the general control framework, I focus much of the discussion on what seem to be three of the most important control-related choices managers must make. First is what type of controls to use and emphasize. Second is when and how to implement a "tight" control system. Third is how to measure performance given that it has been decided to control behavior by holding people accountable for the results they produce; this last issue is singled out for an in-depth treatment because results control is the dominant form of control at managerial levels in most business firms.

The primary intended audience for the book is anyone who is, or who will be, a manager; these are the people who will be responsible for implementing and operating sets of controls. I have attempted to make the book as readable as possible by avoiding the technical jargon that pervades the research literatures and by providing many examples to make the concepts less abstract. I hope that these efforts help further the communication of the ideas so that readers can move easily from them to a constructive redirection of their own efforts.

My thinking in this area has been developing over a four year period, and I am grateful to many who have helped me along the way toward completion of this work. Many of my colleagues at the Harvard Business School have read early manuscript drafts and contributed ideas and examples. They included Francis J. Aguilar, Robert N. Anthony, Thomas V. Bonoma, William J. Bruns, Jr., John Dearden, Julie H. Hertenstein, James L. McKenney, F. Warren McFarlan, Krishna G. Palepu, Thomas R. Piper, and Richard F. Vancil. Others who contributed were Eric G. Flamholtz, University of California, Los Angeles; Vijayaraghavan Govindarajan, Ohio State University; Anthony Hopwood, London Business School; David T. Otley, University of Lancaster; and Srinivasan Umapathy, Boston University. Many managers with whom I have talked contributed ideas and examples. And many students to whom I subjected early versions of these ideas also have made valuable suggestions. I also wish to thank the Division of Research at the Harvard Business School for providing me the time to work on this project and the funding to gather ideas from field sites. Of course, I accept full responsibility for the finished product, including whatever flaws remain.

chapter one

CONTROL: PROBLEMS AND SOLUTIONS

Control, which essentially means "keeping things on track," ranks as one of the critical functions of management. Consistent with its importance, many articles and books about control fill the management literature. For example, in just the last few years companies have been singled out for having "inadequate controls,"[1] for having "tightened up" their controls,[2] for having "loosened up their controls,"[3] for having "simultaneous tight-loose controls,"[4] or for having control systems that stifle creativity and engender a short-term focus on the part of their managers.[5]

Despite the volume of literature, however, control is still a relatively poorly understood part of the management function. A number of problems have impeded progress and understanding. One problem stems from the lack of a comprehensive, generally accepted control framework with supporting terminology. Control systems have been described by various authors as being, for example, administrative, interpersonal, formal, unitary, intuitive, rigid, bureaucratic, meritocratic, and/or paternalistic, and these terms are very difficult to compare and contrast.[6] A second problem is that the control problems and solutions are discussed at different levels of analysis, such as control of inventory (an asset), production (a function), quality (a performance characteristic), salespeople (a role), white-collar crime (specific deviant behaviors), and entire organizations. Third, the solutions that are proposed are also different, as control-related articles may focus on, for example, principles of supervision, motivation, rules and procedures, measurement and reporting, or what auditors have labeled *internal control*. Finally, some authors emphasize that controls deal only with facts about events in the past,[7] whereas others emphasize equally strongly that controls are present and future oriented.[8]

All of these fragments of knowledge are relevant to the understanding of control in organizations, and the fact that the existing knowledge has not been well integrated suggests that there is much work to be done. The potential payoffs — in terms of improved practice — are large. For example, it is often observed that more controls do not necessarily give more control,[9] but the reasons why this occurs are not clear. There is not even a consensus about what controls are intended to do or how to assess how well the objective — which, by definition, must be good control — has been achieved.

This book attempts to tie many of the control-related insights together in a broad discussion of what is known about the management function of control. A new control framework is presented that is useful for relating the major control problems, alternatives, and issues. Among the important questions that are addressed are:

1. Why do managers have to implement controls?
2. What does it mean to have "good" control?
3. What control alternatives exist, and how should managers choose from among the alternatives?
4. What makes a control system tight or loose? Is it desirable to have simultaneous tight-loose controls, and if so, how is that accomplished?
5. What can go wrong if a system of controls is designed or implemented improperly?

It is important to begin with a definition of control and a description of the scope of this book.

CONTROL: WHAT IT IS AND WHAT IT ISN'T

The various functions and tasks managers must perform can be classified and analyzed in many different ways. One common classification scheme separates these functions along a management process continuum that involves objective setting, strategy formulation, and control. While no distinct separation exists between these functions, and there is no general agreement as to where the boundaries between them should be drawn, it is agreed that control is the final function in the management process; it is also clear that this way of looking at management is useful, as "the subject of management controls is one of the oldest in the field of administration."[10]

To limit the scope of this book slightly, control is discussed with the assumption that the *objectives* of the organization in question have already been decided upon. Knowledge of objectives is a necessary prerequisite for conscious control efforts, as without it, activity can only be described as aimless.[11] Objectives do not have to be defined in specific, measurable terms (for example, return on equity), but it is critical to have a general understanding of what the organization is trying to accomplish.

In business organizations (as opposed to, for example, not-for-profit organizations), this is not a very limiting assumption because some understanding of objectives usually exists. Unanimous agreement as to how to balance the responsibilities to the various stakeholders (such as, shareholders, employees, customers, suppliers) is rarely present, but it is usually relatively easy for the owners, or a dominant management coalition, to dictate the areas in which results are expected and how conflicts are to be resolved, such as through bargaining techniques.[12]

Strategy is seen as related to, but usually separable from, control. It is widely recognized that firms with reasonable strategies can fail, or at least have operating difficulties, because of a poor control system. For example, a $21 million embezzlement discovered in early 1981 at Wells Fargo Bank resulted from a control, not a strategy, failure.[13] The converse also happens; that is, firms with good controls can suffer because of poor strategies. Continental Bank of Illinois is an example, as the bank made a bad strategic decision to enter an area of business that it did not understand very well. The bank suffered large losses on property loans in the United Kingdom even though it had "strict controls on the amount of lending and on all quantifiable items."[14]

Strategy, then, is seen as a useful, but not necessary, guide to managers who are attempting to guide and control their organizations. As will be shown later, the better a strategy is formulated, the greater the number of control alternatives that are feasible and the easier it is to implement each alternative effectively. However, it is possible to design and operate some types of controls without having any clear strategies in mind.

Note that not all authors use this approach of treating strategies and the processes used to develop them as distinguishable from control. Some authors include some of the strategic planning processes — those related to deciding if and when strategies need to be changed — as an integral part of control,[15] and others consider the strategic planning processes as conceptually different from control processes but, for all practical purposes, inseparable.[16] This book takes probably the most common approach of considering strategy formulation and evaluation processes to be relevant but outside the main focus of discussion.[17] As will be shown, it is possible to draw this distinction between planning and control and still make many useful observations about control.

Control is seen as having one basic function: to help ensure the proper behaviors of the people in the organization. These behaviors should be consistent with the organization's strategy, if one exists, which, in turn, should have been selected as the best path to take toward achievement of the organization's objectives.

This is a broad conceptualization of control. A diverse set of control devices must be considered, including direct supervision, measurements and rewards, and selection and development of personnel. This conceptualization of control is similar to, but in some ways broader than, what is known in the business policy literature as *strategy implementation;*[18] it is broader because strategy implementation is necessary only after a strategy has been established, whereas controls are necessary, and feasible, even in the absence of a well-defined strategy.

CONTROLS INFLUENCE BEHAVIORS

Control, as the word applies to a function of management, involves influencing human behavior, because it is people who make things happen in an organization. In other words, control involves managers taking steps to help ensure that human beings do what is best for the organization. Controls are necessary to guard against the possibilities that people will do something the organization does not want them to do or fail to do something that they should do.

This behavioral orientation is one area of agreement in the management control literature. For example, a 1956 American Accounting Association committee observed that cost concepts for control serve three main purposes: communication, motivation, and performance appraisal; a member of the committee elaborated on the thinking behind this observation in a later article:

> We [the committee] asked ourselves: "What does the control process actually consist of?" Most authorities agree that control, in the sense in which it is used in business management, has to do with the attempts of one person to direct or influence the actions of other persons. This personal human element in the process came to be the central focus in our thinking.
>
> Although the management control process is often compared with mechanical or electrical control devices, such as the thermostat, such an analogy is apt to be quite misleading. A thermostat reacts to stimuli in a definite, predictable fashion. . . . Human beings, on the other hand, do not behave so predictably. . . . A management control system, which does involve human beings — indeed whose only purpose is to influence the actions of human beings — is therefore fundamentally different from mechanical or electrical controls. Our [early committee] attempt to examine a

control system in terms of its mechanics . . . was bound to fail because it missed the main point entirely. And as soon as we considered the management control process as something that basically involved people and the reactions of people, it became evident that there were some useful things that could be said.[19]

This observation has been reiterated many times since. For example, Edward Lawler and John Rhode observed that

the crucial aspect of any control system is its effect on behavior. . . . The system needs to be designed in a way that assists, guides, and motivates management to make decisions and act in ways that are consistent with the overall objectives of the organization.[20]

Eric Flamholtz defined an *organizational control system* as "a set of mechanisms which are designed to increase the probability that people will behave in ways that lead to the attainment of organizational objectives."[21] Charles Horngren noted:

[Control] systems exist primarily to improve the collective decisions within an organization. Because most decisions entail human behavior, our emphasis rightly belongs on human rather than technical considerations.[22]

Kenneth Euske observed that "possibly the most important aspect of management control is that it is concerned with people in organizations."[23] And Chris Argyris noted that while it may not always be acknowledged, a set of assumptions about what causes human behavior is implicit in the design of any control system.[24]

The key point is that if all personnel could always be relied upon to do what is best for the organization, there would be no need for a control system. But individuals are sometimes unable or unwilling to act in the organization's best interest; so management must take steps to guard against the occurrence, and particularly the persistence, of undesirable behaviors and to encourage desirable behaviors.

THE ROOTS OF CONTROL PROBLEMS

Given this behavioral focus of controls, the next logical question to ask is, What is it about the people on whom the organization must rely that creates the needs for managers to implement controls? The causes of the needs for control, which will be referred to as *control problems,* can be classified into three main categories: lack of direction, motivational problems, and personal limitations.

Lack of Direction

One control problem is that people often lack direction because they do not know what is expected of them. Where this occurs, the likelihood of satisfactory activity occurring is small, of course; so we can say that control systems include everything that managers do to inform each individual as to how to maximize his or her contribution to overall organizational goals.

Motivational Problems

Even where all involved individuals clearly understand what they are expected to do, some choose not to perform as the organization would have them perform because of motivational problems. Motivational problems are common because individual goals and organizational goals do not naturally coincide; in the terminology that is often used in textbooks, there is *lack of goal congruence.*

Employee theft is an obvious example of a problem caused by lack of goal congruence, and estimates suggest that it is a very serious problem. One estimate, by Randolph D. Brock III, the president of Brock International Security Corp. was that

> between 10 and 20 percent of a company's employees will steal anything that isn't nailed down. Another 20 percent will never steal. They would say it is morally wrong. The vast majority of people are situationally honest. They won't steal if there are proper controls.[25]

Another estimate was that 50 percent of all employees steal to some degree; 25 percent take important items; 8 percent steal in volume.[26] And, indeed, in a recent study 76 percent of a sample of workers who were given a polygraph test admitted involvement in employee theft.[27]

These sizable estimates of the percentage of people who cannot always be trusted may, unfortunately, be accurate. Estimates of U.S. losses from white-collar crime alone range from $50 billion[28] to $200 billion a year.[29]

Crime is not the only problem caused by the lack of goal congruence, of course. Legal, but inappropriate, decisions that are simply not in the organization's best interest — such as overspending on management perquisites — are probably many more times more costly in total. For example, a recent study of employees in three industry sectors (retail, hospital, electronics) found that more than two thirds engaged in counterproductive activities such as long lunches, use of sick leaves when not sick, and use of drugs on the job.[30] In fact, simply wasting time was estimated to have cost U.S. employers $125 billion in 1982.[31] Controls are needed to protect the organization against such behaviors.

Personal Limitations

The final behavioral problem that controls must address occurs where people, owing to certain personal limitations, are simply unable to do a good job. Many of these limitations are person specific. They may be caused by a lack of requisite intelligence, training, experience, or information (or other necessary job supports) for the tasks at hand. For example, some of the major operating problems suffered at the Social Security Administration, which resulted in erroneous and tardy checks to recipients, were blamed on a "chronic lack of trained computer technicians."[32] And it has long been recognized that people sometimes get promoted above their level of competence; where this occurs, problems are quite likely to result.

Another common limitation is lack of information. All firms need information about the external environment in order to be able to adapt to it. And in all but the smallest organizations, much intraorganizational exchange of information is necessary so that a coordinated effort can be maintained. Much of this information exchange takes place during formal planning and budgeting processes, and this is one reason why these processes are discussed in detail in texts that deal with the topic of control systems.[33]

Many control problems can be diagnosed as being brought about because key personnel did not have the information necessary to do a good job. For example, Osborne Computer was criticized for having poor controls because, among other things, management "didn't know how much inventory they had [and] they didn't know how much they were spending."[34] The new management at American Bakeries described the company as being in a "state of disarray" because of the absence of critical information about delivery routes, depots, bakeries, and divisions.[35] And some major firms in the romance novel publication industry were recently described as being "out of control" because the key managers in the firms did not have the information necessary to make good publication decisions, and costly mistakes were being made.[36]

Other limitations are innate to all humans. Even the most talented people are unable to perform some duties or to make some judgments. A significant and growing body of psychological research has demonstrated that all individuals — even very intelligent, well-trained, experienced individuals — have some severe limitations on their abilities to perceive new problems, to remember important facts, and to process new information properly.[37] For example, in looking at the future it has been shown that people tend to overestimate the likelihood of most-likely events and events that have occurred relatively recently (both of which are easier to remember) as compared with relatively rare events and those that have not occurred recently. Sometimes training can be used to reduce the severity of these limitations; but in most situations multiple biases and limitations remain, and they are a problem because they reduce the probability that correct decisions will be made or even that the problems will be observed. The control implications of these limitations are just beginning to be explored.

These three control problems — lack of direction, motivational problems, and personal limitations — can obviously occur simultaneously. A person in a job may not understand what is expected, may not be motivated to perform well, and may not be capable of performing well even if he or she understands what is being asked for and is highly motivated to achieve it.

PROBLEM AVOIDANCE

The control problems must be addressed, but what are commonly known as controls are not always the best solution: Sometimes the problems can be avoided. *Avoidance* means eliminating the possibility that the control problems will cause the organization harm. Total avoidance is rare, but partial avoidance can often be achieved by limiting exposure to certain types of problems or to a smaller number of problem sources (that is, particular persons, groups). It can also be achieved by reducing the maximum potential loss if the problems occur. Three avoidance strategies are discussed below: elimination, automation, and risk sharing.

Elimination

Managers can sometimes avoid the control problems associated with a particular entity or activity by turning over the potential profits, and the associated risks, to a third party through such mechanisms as subcontracts, licensing agreements, or divestment. This form of avoidance can be called *elimination*.

Elimination is typically utilized by managers who are not able to control certain activities, perhaps because they do not have the required resources or because they do not have a good understanding of the required processes. For example, General Motors (GM) recently turned its Clark, New Jersey, roller-bearing plant over to the plant's employees. GM management admitted that they had been unable to make the plant perform within acceptable limits with the solutions available to them, and they hoped that the competitive market forces the new firm would face would bring about the necessary productivity changes.[38]

When companies do not wish to avoid completely an area they cannot control well, they are wise at least to limit their investments, and hence their risks, in that area. For example, Chase Manhattan Bank was recently left with a potential $135 million after-tax write-off because of its involvement in the government-securities lending business with Drysdale Government Securities, Inc. In retrospect, bank executives admitted that they did not understand this business and its risks very well and that they had not been wise to become so heavily involved in it.[39] Limiting risk is partial avoidance of problems that might arise.

Automation

A second avoidance possibility is automation. Computers, robots, and other means of automation can sometimes be used to reduce an organization's exposure to some control problems because they can be set to behave appropriately (that is, as the organization desires); and when they are operating properly, they usually perform more consistently than do humans.

> The computer essentially eliminates the problems of accuracy, consistency, and motivation. The computer is immeasurably more accurate than any person performing the same calculations and, once programmed, will be absolutely consistent in its treatment of transactions. Finally, the computer itself will never have any dishonest or disloyal motivations.[40]

In most managerial situations, however, automation can provide only a partial control solution, at best. One limitation is feasibility, as humans have many talents that no machines nor decision models, even the so-called expert systems, have been able to duplicate.[41] A second limitation is cost. Automation often requires major investments that may be justifiable only if improvements in productivity, as well as in control, are forthcoming. Finally, automation may just replace some control problems with others. With computer automation, for example, control risks often increase because the elimination of source documents can obscure the audit trail, and the concentration of information in one location increases security risks.[42]

Risk Sharing

A third (partial) avoidance possibility is risk sharing. Sharing risks with outside entities can bound the losses (or foregone opportunities) that could be incurred by inappropriate employee behaviors. Risk sharing can involve buying insurance against certain undesirable occurrences. For example, many companies purchase fidelity bonds on employees in sensitive positions to reduce the firm's exposure to control problems in these positions. Joint ventures are another way to share risks with outside parties.

These avoidance alternatives are often an effective partial solution to many of the control problems managers face. It is rarely possible to avoid all risk because firms are rewarded for bearing risk, but most firms use some forms of avoidance, automation, and risk sharing in order to bound their areas of exposure to the control problems.

CONTROLS AND CONTROL

For the control problems that cannot be avoided, and those for which decisions have been made not to avoid, managers must (or probably should) implement one or more types of mechanisms that are generally called *controls*. Controls are necessary to ensure that the organization is protected against the deleterious effects of the control problems that have not been avoided. The collection of control mechanisms that are used is generally referred to as a *control system*.

Impossibility of Achieving Perfect Control

The object of a control system is good control. Perfect control does not exist except perhaps in very unusual circumstances. Perfect control would require complete assurance that all individuals on whom the organization must rely always act in the best way possible, or at least in a way that is consistent with the organization's strategy.[43] This is obviously not a realistic expectation because it is virtually impossible to install controls so well designed that they guarantee good behaviors. Furthermore, as controls are costly, it is rarely, if ever, cost effective to try to implement enough controls even to approach perfect control. The reasonable goal, then, is good control.

Good Control and Its Characteristics

Good control means that an informed person can be reasonably confident that no major, unpleasant surprises will occur. The label *out of control* is used to describe a situation where there is a high probability of forthcoming poor performance, despite a reasonable operating strategy.

Some important characteristics of this desirable state of good control should be highlighted. First, control is future oriented; the goal is to have no unpleasant surprises in the future. The past is not relevant except as a guide to the future.

Second, control is multidimensional, and good control is not established over an activity or entity with multiple objectives unless performance on all significant dimensions has been considered. Thus, for example, control of a production department cannot be considered good unless all of its major performance dimensions, including efficiency, quality, and asset management, are well controlled.

Third, the assessment of whether good control has been achieved is difficult and subjective. An informed expert may make a judgment that the control system in place is adequate because no major, unpleasant surprise is likely; but this judgment is subject to error, not only because the expert possesses innate human limitations and biases but also because adequacy must be measured against a future that can be very difficult to predict. As difficult as this assessment of control is, however, it should be done because organizational success depends on a good control system.

Finally, better control — meaning tighter assurances of success — is not always economically desirable. Like any other economic good, the control tools are costly and should be implemented only if the expected benefits exceed the costs. Some economists[44] define the term *control loss* to be the cost of not having a perfect control system; that is, it is the difference between the performance that is theoretically possible, given the strategy selected, and the performance that can be reasonably expected with the control system that is in place. Then it may be said that more or better controls should be implemented only if the amount by which they would reduce the control loss is greater than their cost. Therefore, good control can also be said to have been achieved if the control losses are expected to be smaller than the cost of implementing more controls.

Control systems serve a critical organizational function. If a control system is not in place, or if the system in place is not implemented well, severe repercussions can result. At a minimum, inadequate control can result in lower performance and/or higher risk. At the extreme, if performance is not controlled on one or more critical performance dimensions, the result can be organizational failure.

CONTROL SYSTEM VARIABILITY

In all but very unusual settings, not all of the control problems can be avoided; so management must implement one or more controls to protect the organization against the potential costs of the control problems. A broad range of controls exist, and we can observe that the controls in use vary considerably among companies and among the areas of any single company. For example, as will be shown later, the control system of some firms consists primarily of trying to hire people who can be relied upon to serve the firm well. Other firms provide modest performance-based incentives, and still others offer incentives that can more than double base salaries. Some firms assign the incentives based on the accomplishment of targets defined in terms of financial accounting numbers; others use nonfinancial measures of performance; and still others evaluate performance only subjectively. Some firms have elaborate sets of policies and procedures that they expect all, or maybe some, employees to follow, whereas others have no such procedures or they allow the procedures that were once in place to get out of date. Some firms make extensive use of a large, highly professional internal audit staff, while others do not even have an internal audit function.

These are just examples. The distinctions that can be made among the control systems in use are many, and they are to be expected for several reasons. One reason is that some controls are not feasible in certain situations. The information needed to implement them might not be available, or they might just cost too much. A second reason is that the companies and areas face a different mix of control problems, and some types of controls are better at addressing particular types of problems. A third reason is that some types of controls have some undesirable side effects that can be particularly dangerous in some settings; therefore, they have to be avoided. And finally, since more than one good control alternative is available in many situations, managers can often select the alternatives that best suit their management styles. All of these situations are discussed in later chapters.

CONCLUSION AND OVERVIEW

This chapter has provided an introduction to the subject of control which, in an organizational setting, involves influencing people to behave as the organization would have them behave. It has been argued that inappropriate behaviors can result from any of three types of potential problems: lack of direction, motivational problems, and personal limitations. Managers have a number of possible responses to the presence of these problems. They can avoid some problems, either completely or partially, such as by eliminating or automating a particular activity or by sharing the risk with a joint venture partner or an insurance company.

But avoidance is rarely sufficient by itself; managers must usually implement a system of controls, and control system analysis and design is the focus of the rest of the book.

The next three chapters describe one useful way of looking at the main control alternatives; the controls are classified according to the object of control — that is, whether the focus of the control is on results, actions, or personnel.[45] Chapter 5 examines one of the major determinants of the choice of controls: feasibility. Chapter 6 discusses another major control choice that managers must make: the choice between tight and loose controls; the chapter provides definitions for these terms and shows how the control alternatives can be used, individually and in combination, to produce tighter or looser control. Chapter 7 contains a general discussion of some of the unintended and harmful side effects that controls can cause if they are implemented in the wrong situation and/or used improperly. Chapter 8 describes in detail the unique advantages of financial accountability controls, which involve holding someone accountable for results defined in financial (monetary) terms, and some of the issues that can arise when they are used; the financial controls are singled out for a more detailed discussion because they are probably the most important type of control used at managerial levels in business organizations. Finally, Chapter 9 provides an overview of some of the key considerations managers must face in designing control systems and in analyzing the systems that are in use.

NOTES

1. See, for example, Verbatim Corporation, in Kathleen K. Wiegner, "The One That Almost Got Away," *Forbes,* January 31, 1983, pp. 46–47.
2. See, for example, Allied Corporation, in "The Hennessy Style May Be What Allied Needs," *Business Week,* January 11, 1982, p. 126.
3. See, for example, Gould, Inc., in "Gould Loosens Up as It Gains in High-Tech, But Some Doubt Strong Chief Will Let Go," *Wall Street Journal,* May 26, 1983, p. 33.
4. See, for example, 3M Corporation, in Thomas J. Peters and Robert H. Waterman, Jr., *In Search of Excellence* (New York: Harper & Row, 1982).
5. A general criticism of large U.S. corporations that appears in Robert H. Hayes and William J. Abernathy, "Managing Our Way to Economic Decline," *Harvard Business Review* 58 (July-August 1980): 67–77; and "Big Business Tries to Imitate the Entrepreneurial Spirit," *Business Week,* April 18, 1983, pp. 84–89.
6. For an overview of the control-related research literature, see Kenneth A. Merchant, "Control in Organizations: A Literature Review," Working Paper no. 83–69, (Graduate School of Business Administration, Harvard University, 1983).
7. Peter F. Drucker, *Management: Tasks, Responsibilities, Practices* (New York: Harper & Row, 1974), p. 494.

8. See, for example, Edward E. Lawler III and John G. Rhode, *Information and Control in Organizations* (Pacific Palisades, Calif.: Goodyear, 1976).

9. See, for example, Drucker, *Management*.

10. Leonard Sayles, "The Many Dimensions of Control," *Organizational Dynamics* 1 (Summer 1972): 21.

11. This point was emphasized in both Russell Stout, Jr., *Management or Control?: The Organizational Challenge* (Bloomington: Indiana University Press, 1980), p. 14; and David T. Otley and Anthony J. Berry, "Control, Organization and Accounting," *Accounting, Organizations and Society* 5 (1980): 231–46.

12. For example, see Geert H. Hofstede, "Management Control of Public and Not-for-Profit Activities," *Accounting, Organizations and Society* 6 (1981): 193–216.

13. See, for example, "Fraud at Wells Fargo Depended on Avoiding Computer's Red Flags," *Wall Street Journal,* February 26, 1981, p. 1.

14. David Mitchell, *Control without Bureaucracy* (London: McGraw-Hill, 1979), p. 6.

15. For example, this process is called "strategic control" in Carter F. Bales, "Strategic Control: The President's Paradox," *Business Horizons* (August 1977): 17–28; Peter Lorange, "Strategic Control: Some Issues in Making It Operationally More Useful" (Paper presented at the First European Conference on Corporate Planning, Fontainbleau, France, June 24, 1980); and Charles H. Roush and Ben C. Ball, Jr., "Controlling the Implementation of Strategy," *Managerial Planning* (November-December 1980): 3–12.

16. For example, see Robert N. Anthony, *Planning and Control Systems: A Framework for Analysis* (Boston, Division of Research, Graduate School of Business Administration, Harvard University, 1965).

17. This approach is in evidence in many control-related works. For example, Daniel described the differences between planning data and control data in Donald R. Daniel, "Management Information Crisis," *Harvard Business Review* (September-October 1961): 117–21; Drucker, *Management,* p. 499, observed that "controls follow strategy"; and Euske included a discussion of the "differences between planning and control" in Kenneth J. Euske, *Management Control: Planning, Control, Measurement, and Evaluation* (Reading, Mass.: Addison-Wesley, 1984).

18. For example, see Joseph L. Bower, "Solving the Problems of Business Policy," *Journal of Business Strategy* 2 (Winter 1982): 32–44.

19. Robert N. Anthony, "Cost Concepts for Control," *Accounting Review* 32 (April 1957): 229–30.

20. Lawler and Rhode, *Information and Control,* p. 6.

21. Eric Flamholtz, "Behavioral Aspects of Accounting/Control Systems," in *Organizational Behavior,* ed. Steven Kerr (Columbus, Ohio: Grid, 1979), p. 290.

22. Charles T. Horngren, *Cost Accounting: A Managerial Emphasis* (Englewood Cliffs, N.J.: Prentice-Hall, 1982), p. 318.

23. Euske, *Management Control,* p. 2.

24. Chris Argyris, *Personality and Organization* (New York: Harper & Row, 1957).

25. Dan Gillmor, "Crime Is Headed Up — And So Is Business," *Boston Globe,* February 15, 1983, p. 47.

26. Mark Lipman, *Stealing: How America's Employees Are Stealing Their Companies Blind* (New York: Harper's Magazine Press, 1973).

27. R. R. Schmidt, "Executive Dishonesty: Misuse of Authority for Personal Gain," in *Internal Theft: Investigation and Control,* ed. Sheryl Leininger (Los Angeles: Security World, 1975), pp. 69–81.

28. William McGowan, "The Great White-Collar Crime Coverup," *Business and Society Review* 45 (Spring 1983): 25–31.

29. W. Steve Albrecht and Marshall B. Romney, "Deterring White-collar Crime in Banks," *Banker's Magazine* 163 (November-December 1980): 60–64.

30. Richard D. Hollinger and John P. Clark, *Theft by Employees* (Lexington, Mass: Lexington Books, 1983).

31. "Time Stealing," *Forbes,* December 20, 1982, p. 9.

32. John J. Fialka, "Ailing Computers Give Social Security System Another Big Problem," *Wall Street Journal,* October 5, 1981, p. 1.

33. For example, see Robert N. Anthony and John Dearden, *Management Control Systems* (Homewood, Ill.: Richard D. Irwin, 1980).

34. Erik Larson and Ken Wells, "Shaken Osborne Computer Seeking Suitor in the Face of Possible Failure," *Wall Street Journal,* September 12, 1983, p. 35.

35. "American Bakeries: A New Chef Cleans Up the Kitchen," *Business Week,* June 27, 1983, p. 52.

36. "Why Book Publishers Are No Longer in Love with Romance Novels," *Business Week,* December 5, 1983, p. 157.

37. For example, see summaries by Richard E. Nisbett and Lee Ross, *Human Inference: Strategies and Shortcomings of Social Judgment* (Englewood Cliffs, N.J.: Prentice-Hall, 1980); Robert Libby, *Accounting and Human Information Processing: Theory and Applications* (Englewood Cliffs, N.J.: Prentice-Hall, 1981); and Robert H. Ashton, *Human Information Processing in Accounting,* Studies in Accounting Research no. 17 (Sarasota, Fla.: American Accounting Association, 1982).

38. Allan Sloan, "Go Forth and Compete," *Forbes,* November 23, 1981, pp. 41–42.

39. Julie Salamon, "How New York Bank Got Itself Entangled in Drysdale's Dealings," *Wall Street Journal,* June 11, 1982, p. 1.

40. Paul Hooper and John Page, "Internal Control Problems in Computer Systems," *Journal of Systems Management* 33 (December 1982): 22.

41. See, for example, Richard A. Shaffer, "Simulating Human Thought in Computers Proving Elusive," *Wall Street Journal,* August 5, 1983, p. 23.

42. See, for example, "Experts Say Computerization Raises Risk of Embezzlement," *Wall Street Journal,* February 28, 1981, p. 25.

43. Having perfect control does not necessarily mean that all individuals will act in the organization's best interest, however, because the organization's strategy may be faulty.

44. For example, see Oliver E. Williamson, *Corporate Control and Business Behavior: An Inquiry into the Effects of Organization Form on Enterprise Behavior* (Englewood Cliffs, N.J.: Prentice-Hall, 1970).

45. In some ways this classification scheme is similar to Ouchi's differentiation between

"behavior," "output," and "clan" control; see William G. Ouchi, "A Conceptual Framework for the Design of Organizational Control Mechanisms," *Management Science* 25 (September 1979): 833–48. Some major differences do exist, however, as will become apparent.

chapter two

RESULTS CONTROLS

If asked to think about controls in business organizations, in the United States at least, most people would probably think first about pay-for-performance. This is a type of control that can be called *results control* because it involves rewarding individuals (or otherwise holding them accountable) for accomplishing particular results or outcomes. It is common for the desired results to be defined in financial terms, such as net income, earnings per share, or return on assets, but they can also be defined in nonfinancial terms, such as market share, growth (in units), or the timely accomplishment of certain tasks.

The implementation of results control requires the following three steps: (1) defining the dimension(s) on which results are desired (or not desired), such as earnings per share, product reliability, or level of customer satisfaction; (2) measuring performance on these dimensions; and (3) providing rewards (or punishments) to encourage (or discourage) the behaviors that will lead to those results. The rewards need not be so-called extrinsic rewards (for example, pay, performance), as even without the promise of rewards, people will often motivate themselves to accomplish what is expected of them.[1]

THE INCIDENCE OF RESULTS CONTROLS

At middle- and upper-management levels in most large business organizations, results control is the dominant form of control. Many authors have observed that results control is consistent with, and even necessary for, the implementation of the decentralized forms of organization which have largely autonomous responsibility centers. For example, in the classic book *My Years with General*

Motors,[2] Alfred P. Sloan observed that he was looking for a method by which he could exercise effective control over the whole corporation yet maintain a philosophy of decentralization. At General Motors (and numerous other organizations that followed), the answer was results control, built, for many years, on the return–on–investment (ROI) performance indicator. By using this type of control system, upper management could review and judge the effectiveness of the various organizational entities while leaving the actual execution of operations to those held responsible for the performance of those entities.

Coca-Cola and Westinghouse Electric are two companies that have recently gone through the process of instituting a more decentralized form of organization, with an increased emphasis on results control. Don Keough, Coca-Cola's president, explained his company's intent as follows:

> We're giving our division managers around the world a lot of authority, and we're holding them responsible. We aren't going to reward people in the '80's for perfect attendance. We're going to reward them for meeting objectives that they have agreed to. If they meet them, they're going to have money jingling in their pocket; if they don't, somebody else will be given that opportunity.[3]

Douglas Danforth, Westinghouse's vice-chairman, explained his company's intent very similarly:

> We're giving our business units a high degree of autonomy because it is difficult for those of us in the top jobs to orchestrate everything that goes on in these units. [At the same time] we are giving [the business unit managers] a strong sense of accountability by holding them to agreed targets.[4]

At middle levels in many firms, where financial goals to not necessarily predominate, results controls are often implemented under the framework of a management-by-objectives (MBO) system. In its most basic form, MBO is

> a process whereby the superior and subordinate managers of an organization jointly identify common goals, define each individual's major areas of responsibilities in terms of the results expected of them, and use these measures as guides for operating the unit and assessing the contribution of each of its members.[5]

Results control can also be emphasized down to the lowest levels in some parts of the organization, as many companies have done, and with good effects. For example, for many years it has been common for delivery personnel, such as milkmen, to be paid on a commission basis. At Frito-Lay deliverymen receive only a small weekly salary, but they are paid a 10 percent commission on all the chips they sell. Studies have found that this encourages them to serve the company's interest better: the drivers do not merely deliver the chips;

they also "stop to talk with supermarket managers, angling for an extra foot of shelf space."[6]

Porsche, the German automobile manufacturer, and the Lincoln Electric Company use results control down to the lowest organizational levels in their manufacturing areas. Porsche, which is known for high-quality products, enters the name of the worker who installs each major engine component in the engine's log so that if a fault appears later, it can be traced back to the person responsible.[7] Lincoln Electric provides wages based solely on piecework for most factory jobs and liberal performance-related bonuses that can more than double an individual's pay,[8] and this incentive system has created such high productivity that some of the industry giants have found it difficult, or even impossible, to compete in Lincoln's line of business: arc welding. For example, General Electric left the arc-welding business entirely, and Westinghouse has been squeezed into a small corner of the market. A *Business Week* article observed that "in its reclusive, iconoclastic way, Lincoln Electric remains one of the best-managed companies in the U.S. and is probably as good as anything across the Pacific."[9]

RESULTS CONTROLS AND THE CONTROL PROBLEMS

Results controls are effective because they address some of the problems that cause the needs for controls. When they are designed properly, results controls are particularly effective in addressing motivational problems. People are induced to behave so as to maximize their chances of producing the results the organization desires because those results are also, not coincidentally, those that will maximize their own rewards.

Results controls can also be used to inform people as to what is expected of them. Thus, they can be effective in alleviating the potential problem of lack of direction. They are not generally effective in addressing personal limitations.

Results controls should not be confused with what are often referred to as *feedback-* or *cybernetic controls* because results controls are really future oriented. The measurements of past results are made so that the rewards can be assigned to reinforce the promise that more rewards will be forthcoming if future results are satisfactory.

FEASIBILITY OF RESULTS CONTROLS

Although results controls are an important form of control in use in many organizational settings, they cannot be used everywhere. They are feasible only if *all* of the following conditions are present:

1. Knowledge exists as to what results are desirable.
2. The desired result areas can be controlled (at least to some extent) by the individual(s) whose actions are being influenced.
3. The controllable result areas can be measured effectively.

These feasibility conditions are discussed in the following sections.

Knowledge of Desirable Results

For results controls to work, some knowledge must exist as to what results are desirable in the responsibility areas of the person(s) being controlled. In general, a good deal of knowledge about the desired results exists for top management and some lower-level roles but not necessarily for middle-level roles. Knowledge of what results are desirable is adequate for top-level managers because they are responsible for total organizational results, and, as discussed earlier, we can generally assume that for business organizations the overall organizational objectives are known, at least in general terms. Knowledge is also adequate for those lower-level personnel who concentrate on one or on a few relatively well-defined tasks. It is easy to develop results standards for those in highly routinized, standardized jobs as they can be derived from for example, time-and-motion studies, historical comparisons, or cross-person comparisons.

It does not follow, however, that just because the overall organizational objectives are known that the desired results are then also known at all intermediate and lower levels in the organization. The disaggregation of overall organizational objectives into specific expectations for individuals lower in the hierarchy is often very difficult because different needs and trade-offs may be present in different parts of the organization. The following examples illustrate this point.

Purchasing managers are responsible for procuring good-quality materials when needed and at low cost. These three result areas (that is, quality, schedule, cost) can often be traded off against each other, and overall organizational objectives (for example, grow and be profitable) do not provide much help in making these trade-offs because the importance of each of these result areas may vary over time and among parts of the organization, depending on differing needs and strategies. Thus a company short of cash may want to minimize the amount of inventory on hand, and this may make schedule the dominant consideration; a company (or strategic business unit [SBU]) with a lowest–cost producer strategy may want to emphasize the cost considerations; and a company (or SBU) with products with a quality image may emphasize meeting or exceeding specifications of the materials being purchased. To ensure proper purchasing manager behaviors, the orderings of these goals must be made clear.

The development of standards is also difficult for most middle-level general managers. Companies spend considerable time in disaggregating the overall company objectives into individual responsibility areas. This disaggregation is normally carried out during the latter stages of the company's planning and budgeting processes, that is, after the strategic plans have been set, the results targets for specific individuals are established during what are generally called the processes of *programming* and *budgeting*.[10] It is not critical that goals be precise (such as, 15 percent growth in sales), but it is necessary that a general direction of desired performance be determined and that this direction provide guidance as to how the key trade-offs should be made.

Ability to Effect Desirable Results (Controllability)

A second condition that is necessary for results controls to work is that the person whose behaviors are being controlled must be able to effect the desired results in a given time span; that is, the results area must be controllable. This controllability principle — that individuals should not be held accountable for results that they cannot control — appears throughout the control literature.

> A man should be held accountable for only that which he alone can control.[11]

> It is almost a self-evident proposition that, in appraising the performance of divisional management, no account should be taken of matters outside the division's control.[12]

> In deciding which variances to report to a particular manager, we generally apply the *controllability criterion,* that managers should be assigned only those variances they are expected to control.[13]

> A manager is not normally held accountable for unfavorable outcomes or credited with favorable ones if they are clearly due to causes not under his control.[14]

The main rationale behind this control principle, which is rarely highlighted, is that results measurements are useful only to the extent that they provide information about the actions that were taken. If a results area is totally uncontrollable, the results measures tell us nothing about what actions were taken. Partial controllability means that the measures are distorted, and distortion makes it difficult to infer from the results measures whether or not good actions were taken.

Controllability can be illustrated in graphical terms. Assume the general manager of a largely autonomous division is evaluated on some common financial measure of performance (for example, net income) and that he performs exactly as the organization wishes. If everything were controllable, this manager would contribute to the firm at a constant rate (Figure 2.1). Income for the period would be the ending value less the starting value, or $x_1 - x^0$. By looking at this performance measure, it would be possible to infer that the manager had performed appropriately.

Now, instead of everything being totally controllable, assume that two uncontrollable events occurred during the period of time shown in Figure 2.1. First assume that at the end of time period 1 oil is discovered on land entrusted to the manager and that he immediately sells (or is otherwise given credit for) the mineral rights. This fortuitous event would produce a sudden *increase* in the results measure. Then assume that at the end of time period 2 a country in which the manager was compelled by higher management to maintain a plant devalued its currency. This would result in a sudden *decrease* in the economic value of the entity run by the manager whose behaviors we are trying to control.

The resulting performance pattern is shown in Figure 2.2. One would have to conclude that for this period of time, at least, the results area for which

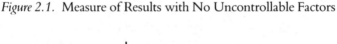

Figure 2.1. Measure of Results with No Uncontrollable Factors

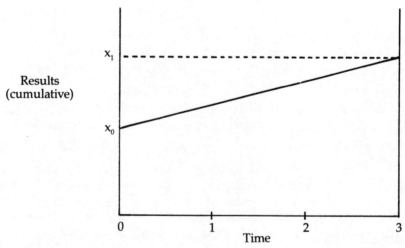

the manager was being held accountable — net income — was largely uncontrollable. If, as has been assumed in Figure 2.2, the effect of the devaluation was greater than the total effect of the oil discovery and the normal value created by the controllable actions, the net income measure for this manager over this time period might show a loss, such as $x_0 - x_2$. Yet this net loss would have occurred despite the fact that the manager was assumed to continue to perform exactly as the organization wished (note the upward-sloping line between the discontinuities).

In the real world, of course, numerous uncontrollable factors affect the measures used to evaluate managerial performance, and these uncontrollable influences hinder efforts to use results reports for control purposes. Instead of a precise measure of performance, often all that can be measured is a broad band within which performance probably lies, as is shown in Figure 2.3, and it becomes very difficult to say whether the results achieved are due to the actions taken or to acts of nature. Good actions will not necessarily produce good results, and bad actions may similarly be obscured.

In cases with many uncontrollable influences on the available results measure(s), results controls are not feasible. Managers cannot be relieved of their responsibility to respond to relevant environmental factors; and if these factors are difficult to track so that their effects can be eliminated from the results measures, results controls are not very effective. The implication, then, should be clear: Where the results that can be measured are not controllable,

Figure 2.2. Measure of Results with Two Uncontrollable Events

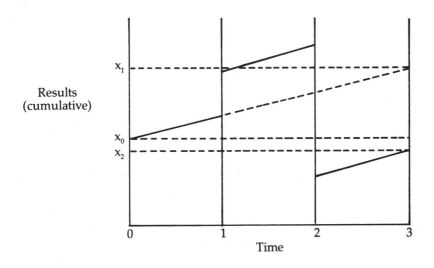

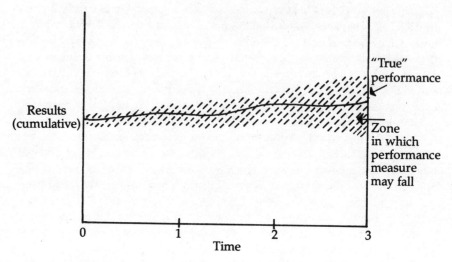

Figure 2.3. Measure of Results with Many Uncontrollable Factors

results control is not feasible; and the effectiveness of results control is inversely related to the importance of the noncontrollable factors that affect the results reports.

Ability to Measure Controllable Results Effectively

The final constraint limiting the feasibility of results control is that often the controllable results that the organization truly desires, and that the individual involved can affect, cannot be measured effectively. Measurement itself is rarely the problem; in virtually all situations *something* can be measured, as, by definition, *measurement* requires only that numbers be assigned to events or objects. But sometimes the key measurements are not feasible.

For example, casinos are unable to measure the results generated by individual dealers of table games such as blackjack, craps, and baccarat. With available technology it is not possible to keep track of each wager made at a table; results are measured only after each shift. But these results do not relate to individual dealers because, owing to the rest breaks that are necessary, more than one dealer works on a table during each shift. So it is not possible to measure the results generated by the personnel in this critical role in casinos.

The more common situation is where some results measures can be generated but they must be judged not to be effective. The one criterion that should be used to judge the effectiveness of results measures is ability to evoke the desired behaviors. This criterion really says nothing about the underlying "veracity" of a results measure (such as, net income): If a measure evokes the right behaviors in a given situation, it is a good control measure; if it does not, it is a bad one, even if it accurately reflects the quantity it purports to represent.

It is possible to use just this one criterion — ability to evoke the right behaviors — to evaluate results measures, but it is useful to decompose this criterion into five criteria for evaluating reports about specific actions. To evoke the right behaviors, results measures should be (1) congruent with true organizational objectives, (2) precise, (3) objective, (4) timely, and (5) understandable.[15] If any of these measurement qualities cannot be achieved, results control will not be effective in evoking the desired behaviors, although for different reasons. The following sections describe each of these qualities and why it is important.

Congruence with True Organizational Objectives

Success in meeting certain organizational objectives often cannot be measured directly, and various surrogate measures (performance indicators) have to be used. The measures used are good only to the extent that they accurately reflect the organization's true objectives, or at least are consistent with the strategy that has been established. This quality can be referred to as *congruence*.[16]

Congruence is obviously an important measurement characteristic because individuals are motivated to do what the control system encourages them to do. If the measures are assessing the wrong things, the wrong behaviors will be evoked.

Precision

Measurement *precision* refers to the amount of randomness or "white noise" in the measure. For precision to be high, the dispersion among the values placed on a given result area by multiple, independent measurers must be small. Precision is an important measurement quality because if measurements are not very precise, neither managers nor subordinates will place much confidence in them.

Some aspects of performance (for example, social responsibility) are difficult, or even impossible, to measure precisely. When precision is low, managers run a higher risk of misevaluating performance and subordinates will react negatively to the inequities that will inevitably arise when equally good performances are rated differently.

Objectivity

Objectivity, which means freedom from bias, is another desirable measurement quality. Measurement objectivity is low — meaning the possibility of biases is high — where either the choice of measurement rules or the actual measuring is done by the persons whose performances are being evaluated. Low objectivity is likely, for example, where performance is self-reported or where managers are allowed considerable discretion in the choice of accounting methods.

Managers have two main alternatives they can use to increase measurement objectivity. They can have the actual measuring done by people who are independent of the process, such as on a controller's staff, or they can have the measurements verified by independent persons, such as auditors. Theoretically, managers could try to cope with the biases by estimating the extent of the biases present and adjusting for them, although because the estimates of the biases would probably be crude, this would inevitably lead to frictions between the parties involved.

Timeliness

Timeliness is an important measurement quality for two reasons. First, if the results measures are not timely, it is not possible to intervene to fix the problems that might exist before they cause potentially severe harm. Second, rewards (or punishments) that must be delayed for significant periods of time lose most of their motivational impact.[17]

Understandability

Two aspects of *understandability* are important. First, the individuals whose behaviors are being controlled must understand what they are to be held accountable for. This requires communication. Sometimes training is also required, as it would be, for example, if managers were to be held accountable for achieving goals expressed in new and different terms, such as inflation-adjusted net income.

Second, the individuals involved must understand what they must do to influence the measure, at least in broad terms. For example, purchasing managers who are held accountable for lowering the costs of purchased materials will not be successful until they develop strategies for accomplishing this goal, such as through improving the negotiations with vendors, increasing competition among vendors, or working with engineering personnel to redesign certain parts. In most situations this is not a limiting factor because when individuals understand what a measure represents, they will figure out what they can do to influence it. In fact, this is one of the advantages of results controls: Managers can accomplish good control without knowing exactly how the results can be brought about.

If a given measure meets these five criteria (congruence, precision, objectivity, timeliness, and understandability), one can safely conclude that the measure will provide an effective basis upon which to base a results control. If they are not met, the measure will not provide a good basis for a results control.

Most measures, however, cannot be classified as either clearly effective or clearly ineffective, and different outcomes will be produced when trade-offs are made between the five comparison criteria. For example, less timely measures can often be made more precise and objective. Thus, in assessing the effectiveness of results measures, many difficult judgments are often necessary. These will be discussed in later chapters.

CONCLUSION

This chapter has provided a brief description of one important form of control — results control — that is used in most organizations and at multiple organizational levels. What makes results controls effective in so many situations is that they can yield good control while simultaneously allowing the people whose behaviors are being controlled high autonomy. And they can even be effective, sometimes, when it is not clear what behaviors are most desirable. But results controls cannot be used in every situation, because failure to satisfy all of the three feasibility conditions — knowledge of desirable results, ability to affect desirable results, and ability to measure controllable results — will render the control ineffective and, probably, precipitate any of a number of dysfunctional side effects, many of which are discussed in later chapters.

When results controls are not feasible, many managers resort to what can be called *action controls*. These are the focus of the next chapter.

NOTES

1. See, for example, Edward E. Lawler III, "Control Systems in Organizations," in *Handbook of Industrial and Organizational Psychology,* ed. Marvin D. Dunnette (Skokie, Ill.: Rand McNally, 1975), pp. 1247–91.
2. Alfred P. Sloan, Jr., *My Years with General Motors* (New York: Doubleday, 1964).
3. John Huey, "New Top Executives Shake Up Old Order at Soft-Drink Giant," *Wall Street Journal,* November 6, 1981, p. 17.

4. "Operation Turnaround," *Business Week,* December 5, 1983, p. 125.

5. George Odiorne, *Management by Objectives: A System of Management Leadership* (Belmont, Calif.: Pitman Learning Inc., 1965), pp. 55–56.

6. Janet Guyon, "The Public Doesn't Get a Better Potato Chip without a Bit of Pain," *Wall Street Journal,* March 25, 1983, p. 1.

7. "Automaking on a Human Scale," *Fortune,* April 5, 1982, pp. 89–93.

8. See, Norman Fast and Norman Berg, "The Lincoln Electric Company," case no. 9–376–028 (Boston: HBS Case Services, 1975); and Maryann Mrowca, "Ohio Firm Relies on Incentive-Pay System to Motivate Workers and Maintain Products," *Wall Street Journal,* August 12, 1983, p. 23.

9. "This Is the Answer," *Business Week,* July 5, 1982, pp. 50–52.

10. See, for example, Richard F. Vancil and Peter Lorange, "Strategic Planning in Diversified Companies," *Harvard Business Review* 53 (January-February 1975): 81–90.

11. Gene W. Dalton, "Motivation and Control in Organizations," in *Motivation and Control in Organizations,* ed. Gene W. Dalton and Paul R. Lawrence (Homewood, Ill.: Richard D. Irwin and the Dorsey Press, 1971). p. 27.

12. David Solomons, *Divisional Performance: Measurement and Control* (Homewood, Ill.: Richard D. Irwin, 1965), p. 83.

13. Gordon Shillinglaw, *Managerial Cost Accounting* (Homewood, Ill.: Richard D. Irwin, 1982), p. 260.

14. Kenneth J. Arrow, "Control in Large Organizations," in *Behavioral Aspects of Accounting,* ed. Michael Schiff and Arie Y. Lewin (Englewood Cliffs, N.J.: Prentice-Hall, 1974), p. 284.

15. This list is similar in nature to, but different from, the qualitative characteristics of financial measures proposed by the U.S. Financial Accounting Standards Board (FASB) Concepts Statement no. 2. (Financial Accounting Standards Board, "Qualitative Characteristics of Accounting Information: Statement of Financial Accounting Concepts no. 2," May 1980.) The differences are necessary because the FASB's list is built using a decision-usefulness perspective; so relevance to particular decisions (such as, investment, lending) is a primary concern. Here the focus is control, which is akin to stewardship (depending on how broadly stewardship is defined), and it is natural that a different list of qualities is important. For a discussion of the differences between accounting for decision making and accounting for accountability (or stewardship), see Yuji Ijiri, "On the Accountability-Based Framework of Accounting," *Journal of Accounting and Public Policy* 2 (Summer 1983): 75–82.

16. In an earlier article by this author, this quality was called *correctness.* See Kenneth A. Merchant, "The Control Function of Management," *Sloan Management Review* 23 (Summer 1982): 43–55. A different label was chosen here to eliminate possible confusion with the veracity quality referred to above. Peter Drucker (*Management: Tasks, Responsibilities, Practices* [New York: Harper & Row, 1974], p. 501) also uses the term *congruence* in this identical context.

17. This observation has been made by many authors. See, for example, Victor H. Vroom, *Work and Motivation* (New York: Wiley, 1964); and, Edward E. Lawler III, *Pay and Organization Development* (Reading, Mass.: Addison-Wesley, 1980).

chapter three

ACTION CONTROLS

Another common type of controls, *action controls,* are used to ensure that individuals perform (or do not perform) certain actions that are known to be beneficial (or harmful) to the organization. Action controls are the most direct form of controls because control involves taking steps to make certain that individuals act in the organization's best interest, and with action controls, it is the actions themselves that are the focus of the controls.

Action controls take four basic forms: behavioral constraints, preaction reviews, action accountability, and redundancy. Each is discussed in the following sections.

BEHAVIORAL CONSTRAINTS

Behavioral constraints are a negative form of action control that involve making it impossible, or at least more difficult, for people to do things that should not be done. Constraints can be applied physically or administratively.

Most companies use multiple forms of physical constraints, including locks on desks, computer passwords, and limits on access to areas where valuable inventories and sensitive information are kept. Some types of behavioral constraint devices are becoming very sophisticated technically, such as magnetic identification-card readers, voice-pattern detectors, and fingerprint readers.

Behavior can also be constrained administratively by placing limits on certain persons' abilities to perform all or a portion of specific acts. One common form of administrative control is *centralization;* this means removing some decision-making autonomy from lower-level individuals. Managers who make all the key decisions in certain areas under their responsibility have solved most of the control problems because no employees are given the opportunity to make costly wrong decisions.

Centralization is the dominant form of control in some companies, as all the key decisions are made at top management levels. This is the case in many small businesses, but it is also true in some large businesses, including Amerada Hess Corporation and Data General Corporation. Amerada Hess's controls are considered tight because its chairman, Leon Hess, is said to run the business "like a family store, with an iron grip on authority."[1] Data General's president, Edson de Castro, also maintains centralized control; a former manager in the company observed that "all the real decisions in that company go to one desk — de Castro's."[2]

Some companies resort to centralization in specific areas at various times in their histories to strengthen control. For example, in late 1982, Tandem Computers, Inc., became aware of "overly aggressive sales practices" and an "apparent lack of accounting controls," which led to a downward restatement of fiscal 1982 results. One of the company's responses was to add a layer of management to centralize the control of manufacturing, product management, and international marketing.[3] Recently, Hewlett-Packard,[4] Apple Computer,[5] and many of the large accounting firms[6] have also centralized certain operations to improve overall company direction and coordination.

To some extent, companies utilize centralization in all functional areas and at all levels of management, as managers tend to reserve many of the most critical decisions that fall within their authority (that is, those with the greatest potential impacts) for themselves. However, in most organizations of even minimal size, it is not possible to centralize all critical activities; so other control solutions are necessary.

Another common form of administrative control is *separation of duties,*[7] which involves dividing up the tasks necessary for the accomplishment of certain sensitive duties. For example, it is generally agreed that the person who makes the payment entries in the accounts receivable ledger should not also receive the checks. A person with both duties could divert the checks to a personal account and cover the action by, perhaps, making fictitious entries of returns of goods or price adjustments. The way to eliminate this risk is to have another employee open the mail, list, endorse, and total incoming checks. If that person diverts checks, the receivables cannot be adjusted to hide the fraud, and customers will eventually complain about being dunned for amounts they have already paid. Such separation of duties is described by auditors as one of the basic requirements of what they call good "internal control."[8]

Proper administrative constraints such as centralization and separation of duties make it impossible or difficult to complete certain tasks that should not be completed. The end result is identical to that of the physical constraints.

PREACTION REVIEWS

A second form of action controls is preaction reviews, which involve observing the work or plans of the individuals being controlled before the activity is complete and making adjustments as necessary. For example, the state enterprise control office in Brazil was recently struggling to bring the giant state companies, including the oil company Petrobras, "under control," and two of its important actions were to review all company budgets in detail and to tell the companies they could not borrow without permission.[9] These are both preaction review controls.

Preaction reviews come in many forms, some formal and some informal. A common form of formal preaction review is a policy of requiring approvals for expenditures of certain types. Most managers are able to spend only a certain amount of money without review by a higher authority, and the review limit often varies by type of expenditure (for example, capital, expense). Another set of formal preaction reviews take place during organizational planning and budgeting processes, as there are usually multiple levels of reviews of planned actions.

Informal reviews of actions are also an important part of most organizations' control systems. They may involve nothing more than a hallway chat between a superior and a subordinate.

Preaction reviews provide control in two basic ways. First, the reviews can eliminate mistakes or other harmful actions before they occur. And second, they can influence behavior just by the threat of the impending review, such as in prompting extra care in the preparation of an expenditure proposal.

ACTION ACCOUNTABILITY

A third form of action control is action accountability, which involves holding employees accountable for their actions. The implementation of action accountability controls requires (1) defining what actions are acceptable (or unacceptable), (2) tracking what happens, and (3) rewarding or punishing deviations from the defined limits. When the desired actions are communicated in written form, action accountability is akin to what organization theorists call "structuring of activities,"[10] and it is the core element in what is labeled as *bureaucratic control*[11] or *administrative control*.[12]

The actions for which people are to be held accountable can be communicated either administratively or socially. Administrative modes of communication include the use of work rules, policies and procedures, contract provisions, or company codes of conduct. For example, it is common in chains of fast-food franchises, such as McDonald's, Wendy's, and Burger King, to prescribe and communicate in writing and through training classes how virtually everything should be done, including how to handle cash, how to hire new employees, and what temperature to keep the grease while cooking french fries. Similarly, department store managers have sets of procedures they are expected to follow; for example, at Sears, Roebuck managers are rebuked if empty merchandise cartons are not broken down before they are sent to the trash room (presumably because employees could use the cartons to steal merchandise).[13]

The actions that are desired do not have to be communicated in written form, of course. They can be communicated through the oral instructions of a superior. And sometimes they are not explicitly communicated at all. For example, in many operational (or performance) audits and peer reviews of auditors, lawyers, doctors, and managers, people are held accountable for actions that were not clearly delineated in advance and that might not even have become recognized as desirable had it not been for the audit or review.[14]

While action accountability controls are most effective if the desired actions are well communicated, communication is not, by itself, enough to make these controls effective. As with results controls, which are also accountability based, the effectiveness of action accountability controls depends on the affected individuals understanding what is required and feeling reasonably sure that their individual actions will be noticed and rewarded or punished in some significant way.

REDUNDANCY

A fourth, relatively minor, form of action control is redundancy. Redundancy involves assigning more people (or machines) to a task than is theoretically necessary, or at least having backup people available, to increase the probability that a task will be accomplished. It is common in computer facilities and other very critical operations but, because of its expense, not in other areas.

ACTION CONTROLS AND THE CONTROL PROBLEMS

Action controls work because they, like the other types of controls, address one or more of the control problems. The behavioral constraints are primarily effective in eliminating motivational problems, as particular individuals who might want to do undesirable things can be prevented from doing so.

The preaction reviews address all of the control problems. Since they may involve communication from the reviewer to the person being controlled, they can help alleviate a lack of direction. They can provide motivation, as people often want to have a carefully thought-out presentation prior to the review. And they can reduce the negative effects of the personal limitations, since the reviewer presumably can add expertise if it is needed.

The action-accountability controls can also address all of the control problems. The definition of desired actions can help provide direction and alleviate the types of personal limitations that are due to inadequate skills or experience. And the rewards or punishments help provide motivation.

Redundancy is the most limited in application. But it can be effective in helping to accomplish a particular task if there is some doubt as to whether the person assigned to the task is capable of getting it done satisfactorily.

FEASIBILITY OF ACTION CONTROLS

While they are a very common form of control in business organizations, action controls cannot be used in every situation. They are feasible only when both of the following conditions exist:

1. Some knowledge exists as to what actions are desirable (or undesirable); and
2. There is an ability to make sure that the desirable actions occur (or that the undesirable actions do not occur).

Knowledge as to What Actions Are Desirable

Lack of knowledge as to what actions are desirable is the constraint that most limits the feasibility of action controls, but the particular actions individuals should perform can be discovered or learned in several ways. One is by analyzing the actions-results patterns of a particular situation, or similar situations, over time to learn what actions produce the best results. A second is by studying what happens to others in similar situations. A third is by being informed by others such as consultants or other experts in the field.

Even though knowledge of what actions are desirable is critical, it is often very difficult to obtain, particularly in certain areas. For example, it may be easy to define relatively completely the actions required on a production line, but the definitions of preferred actions in highly complex and uncertain environments, such as for research engineers or top management, cannot be as complete or as precise.

Lack of knowledge of desirable actions definitely limits the application of action controls. For example, a small manufacturing firm that was considering a change in the controls over its sales function recently faced this knowledge-limitation problem. A consulting firm hired to evaluate the effectiveness of the sales controls recommended implementing an elaborate set of reports to track how the salesmen were allocating their time among types of customers and between direct sales and general market development for action control purposes. The company resisted collecting this information, however, primarily because they did not know how to use it; they did not have a good idea as to how a salesman *should* spend his time, and until that was discovered, they did not consider the information about the actions actually taken to be very useful.[15]

Ability to Ensure That Desired Actions Are Taken

Knowing what actions are desirable is not enough to ensure good control; managers must have some ability to ensure that the desired actions are taken. This ability varies widely among the different action controls.

The behavioral constraints are limited in application in that they work only in a negative sense. That is, they are useful only to help ensure that certain undesirable actions are not taken, as in voluntary organizations (like corporations), it is generally not possible to coerce someone to do something.

Just saying some behavior is not allowable is not enough, however. Management must be able to ensure that unauthorized persons cannot do whatever is intended to be constrained. For example, most firms have centralized the important and technical decisions to enter into foreign currency transactions, but just saying that the authority is centralized does not always preclude unauthorized individuals from getting involved. At Spectra-Physics, a manufacturer of gas lasers, an employee was recently able to enter the company into large foreign-exchange contracts and to conceal the practice from the company; the losses were expected to be approximately $10 million.[16] The identical problem occurred at Dai-Ichi Kangyo Bank, Japan's largest commercial bank. The bank suffered a $36 million loss because of unauthorized foreign-exchange speculation over a recent four-year period in its Singapore branch.[17] Many other similar instances of ineffective behavioral constraints exist.

Behavioral constraints can be set up to be more or less restrictive. In fact, a major portion of the reviews of internal controls in which auditors engage are concerned with looking for situations where the behavioral constraints in place are not effective. In general, more restrictive constraints provide better control, but the cost is usually higher and there may be more significant negative side effects.

Use of redundancy is also limited usually to very specific, low-level tasks. At higher organizational levels, assigning more than one person to the same task usually results in conflict and frustration.

Preaction reviews, on the other hand, are feasible in a broad range of situations. They are limited only by the timely availability of a person (or persons) who understands what actions are desirable.

The analysis of the feasibility of action accountability controls is more complex. Some actions cannot be tracked at all. For example, the management of a small computer company that wanted to monitor the actions of the independent sales representatives through whom they sold their product found that action accountability was not feasible. The representatives resisted the company's requests to report how they spent their time, and the company eventually withdrew its requests.

In most situations, however, some actions can be tracked, and the feasibility analysis then depends on a judgment as to whether the tracking of actions can be done effectively. The criteria that can be used to judge whether the action tracking is effective are very similar to the criteria used to judge the feasibility of results controls: congruence, precision, objectivity, timeliness, and understandability. They are discussed again briefly in this context.

Congruence means that the actions for which the individuals are to be held accountable are in fact the actions that will lead to the highest probability of accomplishment of one or more of the organization's objectives, or at least the proper implementation of the strategy that is being used. For example, dictating a procedure for bank loan officers to follow is only correct if it leads them to perform a superior analysis of a prospective client's ability to pay back the loan.

Precision refers to the amount of error in the indicators used to tell what actions have taken place. In many situations, auditors describe precision of action tracking in terms of the "clarity of the audit trail."

Precision in action tracking is often a limitation. For example, a firm was considering requiring salespeople to spend a certain percentage of their time in market development activities, as opposed to direct sales activities. But this control effort was doomed to failure until precise definitions could be developed as to which actions fell into each of these two areas.[18]

Another precision failure of an action control occurred with the U.S. Foreign Corrupt Practices Act. This act was intended to make significant bribes to foreign officials illegal. But "facilitating payments to lower-level officials" were considered allowable, and the difference between bribes and facilitating payments was not made clear. The vagueness of this law caused, and is causing, much concern among corporate officials who cannot be sure that their interpretations of the provisions of the act would be the same as those independent observers (such as, a jury) might reach at a later date.[19]

Objectivity — freedom from bias — is a concern because reports of actions prepared by those whose actions are being controlled cannot necessarily be relied upon. For example, project-oriented personnel are frequently asked to prepare self-reports of how they spend their time. In most cases, these reports are precise, as the allocations may be in units of time as small as one tenth of an hour. But the reports are not objective; if the personnel involved want to obscure the true time patterns — perhaps to cover a bad performance or to allow some personal time — it is relatively easy for them to report that most of their time was spent on productive activities. Many companies use internal auditors to provide an objectivity check on such reports because without objectivity management cannot be sure whether the action reports reflect the actual actions taken, and they lose their value for control purposes.

Timeliness in tracking actions is important for the same reasons as it is with results measures. If the tracking is not timely, much of the motivational effect of the feedback and rewards is lost, and interventions are not possible.

Finally, it is important that the actions for which individuals are to be held accountable be understandable. The most common *understandability* problem occurs where the action is defined in aggregate terms and the individual involved does not understand the series of steps that are required to achieve the overall result. For example, an auditor who is told to "test an accounts receivable balance" may not understand that his or her test will be judged based on the satisfactory accomplishment of a series of generally accepted steps, including inspections of documentation, confirmations, computations, reconciliations of general-ledger balances, and clerical checks. If these procedures are not understood, the overall behavioral effect will be unsatisfactory even though the aggregate action is defined correctly and the tracking of whether or not the steps have been performed adequately can be done precisely, objectively, and on a timely basis.

While most action-tracking limitations can usually be addressed satisfactorily, in some cases the problems are occasionally severe enough to render action controls impotent. For example, precision problems limit the effectiveness of company codes of conduct, and objectivity is often a problem with tracking actions at remote locations. Implementing action controls where one of these qualities cannot be achieved will lead to some undesirable effects that are discussed in Chapter 7.

CONCLUSION

This chapter has provided an overview of the most direct type of controls: action controls. They are the most direct type of controls because *control* is defined as ensuring the proper actions of the people on whom the organization must rely, and action controls address this objective by focusing on the actions themselves.

Like results controls, action controls are an important part of the control systems used in most organizations and at most organizational levels. Action controls take several different forms: behavioral constraints, preaction reviews, action accountability, and redundancy. But it is useful to discuss them together because they are all focused on the same object of control (actions), and they have the same basic feasibility constraints.

Results controls and action controls usually form the major elements in the control systems used in all but the smallest organizations, but they are usually supplemented by what can be called *personnel controls*. These are the subject of the next chapter.

NOTES

1. Steve Mufson, "Amerada Hess Chief Keeps Controls Tight, Emphasizes Marketing," *Wall Street Journal,* January 11, 1983, p. 1.
2. "Data General's Management Trouble," *Business Week,* February 9, 1981, p. 58.
3. "An Acid Test for Tandem's Growth," *Business Week,* February 28, 1983, p. 64.
4. For example, see Kathleen K. Wiegner, "Back into the Race," *Forbes,* October 10, 1983, pp. 30–32.
5. For example, see Erik Larson and Carrie Dolan, "Once All Alone in Field, Apple Computer Girds for Industry Shakeout," *Wall Street Journal,* October 4, 1983, p. 1.
6. For example, see "As Many of the Big Eight Centralize, Price Waterhouse Bucks the Trend," *Business Week,* October 24, 1983, pp. 114–18.
7. This is sometimes referred to as *segregation of functions*.
8. See, for example, Walter G. Kell and Richard E. Ziegler, *Modern Auditing* (Boston: Warren, Gorham & Lamont, 1980), p. 116.
9. Neil Ulman, "Brazilian Oil Company Has Much of the Clout of Government Itself," *Wall Street Journal,* November 17, 1983, p. 1.
10. For example, see Derek S. Pugh, David J. Hickson, C. R. Hinings, and C. Turner, "Dimensions of Organization Structure," *Administrative Science Quarterly* 15 (1968): 65–105.
11. Max Weber, *The Theory of Social and Economic Organization,* trans. A. M. Henderson and Talcott Parsons (New York: Free Press, 1947).
12. See, for example, John Child, "Strategies of Control and Organizational Behavior," *Administrative Science Quarterly* 8 (March 1973): 1–17; and William J. Bruns, Jr., and John H. Waterhouse, "Budgetary Control and Organization Structure," *Journal of Accounting Research* 13 (Autumn 1975): 177–203.
13. See Vijayarghavan Govindarajan and Joseph G. San Miguel, "Sears, Roebuck and Co. (C): The Internal Audit Function," case no. 9–179–125 (Boston: HBS Case Services, 1979).

14. For example, a report of the Special Committee on Operational and Management Auditing of the American Institute of Certified Public Accountants (American Institute of Certified Public Accountants, *Operational Audit Engagements* [New York: American Institute of Certified Public Accountants, 1982]) listed one of the benefits of an operational audit as "identification of previously undefined organizational policies and procedures." Management may, however, be held accountable for not having had these policies and procedures in place if it is judged that they are part of what might be called "generally accepted management practice," as was the case, for example, with an audit of Portland General Electric Company made by auditors from Arthur D. Little, Inc. See Rajiv D. Banker and Joseph G. San Miguel, "Portland General Electric Company," case no. 9–178–171 (Boston: HBS Case Services, 1978).

15. Kenneth A. Merchant and Thomas V. Bonoma, "Macon Prestressed Concrete Company (A)-(D)," case nos. 9–182–175, 9–182–176, 9–182–177, 9–182–266 (Boston: HBS Case Services, 1982).

16. "Spectra-Physics Sees Fiscal '83 Loss, Cites a $10 Million Charge," *Wall Street Journal,* August 9, 1983, p. 18.

17. "Singapore Slings — and Arrows," *Economist,* October 2, 1982, p. 90.

18. Merchant and Bonoma, "Macon Prestressed Concrete Company (A)-(D)."

19. See, for example, Robert N. Holt and Rebecca E. Fincher, "The Foreign Corrupt Practices Act," *Financial Analysts Journal* 37 (March-April 1981): 73–76; and Laura Landro, "Analysis of ITT's Report Shows Problems in Halting Questionable Foreign Payments," *Wall Street Journal,* June 3, 1982, p. 27.

chapter four

PERSONNEL CONTROLS

Often individuals do, by themselves, what is best for the organization because they are self-directed or because they are influenced by social (group) pressure. Most managers rely on these positive, naturally occurring forces to some extent, and they also take steps to increase the chances that these forces are present and/or that they will produce the appropriate actions. These managerial actions can be called *personnel controls*.

THE FORCES BEHIND PERSONNEL CONTROLS

In using personnel controls, managers are trying to tap and encourage either or both of two basic forces. The first, individual self-control, is a naturally present force that pushes most people to want to do a good job. The second, social control, is a pressure exerted by groups on those who deviate from group norms and values. These will be discussed separately.

Individual Self-Control

Some very powerful types of controls result from the internal motivations of the individuals being controlled, and almost every control system involves some degree of trust that the individuals of concern will do what is best for the organization without any, or with only incomplete, monitoring of actions or results. Most people derive some self-satisfaction from doing a good job and seeing the company succeed. As a consequence, managers can often get good results without adding any obtrusive controls because these inner, personal drives can be strong motivating factors, especially if all the lower-level needs (for example, adequate pay) are satisfied. The phenomena underlying this type of control have been discussed in the management literature under a variety of labels, including "self-control,"[1] "intrinsic motivation,"[2] "ethics and morality,"[3] "trust and atmosphere,"[4] "loyalty,"[5] and "culture."[6]

Social Control

Managers can also encourage people to monitor others' behaviors. It has long been recognized that work groups can influence the behavior of individuals in the group and that the strength of influence depends on factors such as identification with the group, uniformity of group opinion, and group size.[7]

Social control can actually be effected in several directions. It is effected in a top-down direction by superiors' forming particular work groups and encouraging a particular type of organizational culture. It can be effected among peers, as, for example, nonconformers are often under pressure to accept group norms. It can also be effected in a bottom-up direction, as superiors are often pressured to fulfill subordinates' expectations of their role.

ENCOURAGING AND FACILITATING THE POSITIVE FORCES

Where the existing self and social forces cannot be relied on to provide the needed degree of security, management can, in a number of ways, attempt to augment these positive forces in the people on whom they must rely. Five major ways of doing this are discussed in the following sections: (1) selection and placement, (2) training, (3) cultural control, (4) group-based rewards, and (5) provision of necessary resources.

Selection and Placement

Getting the right person to do a particular job can obviously increase the probability that a job will be done right. Firms devote considerable time and effort to selection and placement, and a huge literature has been built up to describe how these tasks should be best accomplished.[8] Much of the literature describes possible predictors of success, such as education, experience, past performances, and personality and social skills. More exotic techniques also exist, as some firms have resorted to analyzing potential employees' handwriting[9] or using polygraph (lie detector) tests[10] to try to weed out high-risk individuals.

Whatever techniques are used, selection and placement are sometimes the single most important elements in some firms' control systems. For example, the founder of Wal-Mart attributed much of his company's prosperity to the company's success in selecting its people.

> Our philosophy is that management's role is simply to get the right people in the right places to do a job and then to encourage them to use their own inventiveness to accomplish the task at hand.[11]

Where it involves assignment of individuals into work groups, placement can also be a way to effect social control. Persons who have one or more of the control problems — lack of direction, motivational problems, and/or personal limitations — can be nurtured, encouraged, and, if need be, chastised by members of the work groups to which they have been assigned, and this may obviate the needs for other forms of controls.

Training

Training is another common way to help employees do a good job. It can provide useful information about what tasks are required and how they can be performed. It might also have positive motivational effects because employees can be given a greater sense of professionalism, and they might be more interested in doing well in a job they understand better.

Many firms use formal training programs — in classroom settings, for example — to improve the skills of their personnel, but much training takes place informally — through mentoring, for example. Jerry Reinsdorf, a successful entrepreneur and current chairman of the Chicago White Sox baseball club, noted the importance of his role as a mentor:

> My management style is to hire good people and develop a relationship with them so that 95% of the time they'll know what decision I'd make and go ahead without asking me.[12]

His control system could be described as being dominated by selection and training, two important forms of personnel controls.

Cultural Control

Some managers encourage self-control by developing a beneficial corporate culture built on shared traditions, beliefs, and values. One author suggested that this might even be considered one of the common elements of successful organizations:

To create an institution we rely on many techniques for infusing day-to-day behavior with long-run meaning and purpose. One of the most important of these techniques is . . . to state . . . what is distinctive about the aims and methods of the enterprise. Successful institutions are usually able to fill in the formula, "What we are proud of around here is . . ."[13]

Cultures have powerful influences on people's behaviors, and they have the advantage of usually being a relatively unobtrusive form of control. The limits of acceptable behaviors may be prescribed in terms as simple as "the way we do things around here."[14] The people whose actions are being controlled may not even think of the shared norms as being part of the organizational control system, but it is clear that organizational cultures (that is, shared values) can substitute for other more formal types of controls. For example, in the course of their interviews, Thomas Peters and Robert Waterman observed that "the stronger the culture . . . the less need there [was] for policy manuals, organization charts, or detailed procedures and rules."[15]

The primary problem with cultural control is that it is very difficult to create a good, strong culture. The best chance seems to be very early in an organization's life, when a founder can imbue the organization with a distinctive culture.[16] But to some extent, strong leaders and management policies added later in an organization's history can also have an impact; in fact, one of the distinguishing traits of strong, effective leaders is that they transmit their values throughout the organization. Culture can also be transmitted through a policy of intraorganizational transfers, as transfers tend to improve the socialization of the individuals in an organization and thereby inhibit the formation of incompatible goals and perspectives. One study of transfers of executives among divisions of multinational firms found that the transfers increased the executives' organizational, as opposed to subunit, identification and gave them a better appreciation of the problems faced by different parts of the organization.[17] One of the keys to success of Japanese firms seems to be their policy of moving managers frequently among functions and divisions to give them a better understanding of the organization as a whole.[18] This approach stands in sharp contrast to the transfer policies of most U.S. firms where managers tend to stay primarily in a single function or single division.

The larger Japanese firms also tend to employ their employees for long periods of time, usually a lifetime. This is another method of increasing the homogeneity of perspectives in an organization.[19]

Group-Based Rewards

Providing rewards based on collective achievement encourages social control. Plans that provide awards for collective performance come in many forms.

Many companies have bonus plans based on corporate or division performance, such as in terms of growth or profits. Other companies encourage broad ownership of company stock so that everyone will share in the company's success. All employees of People Express Airline, Inc., are required to own at least 100 shares of company stock,[20] and those in the new American West Airlines are required to own shares worth 20 percent of their starting salary.[21]

These reward plans are included here as a type of personnel control, rather than as a results control, because they are quite different in character from those that give rewards for individual accomplishment. The link between individual effort and the results being rewarded is very weak; so motivation to achieve the rewards is not the primary force that is effected — social control is. Thus, while these plans have some of the characteristics of results controls, they seem to be designed more for other purposes — to communicate what is expected and to share the wealth that has been created.

Most managers understand this difference very clearly. Graham Sterling, vice-president of Strategic Planning at Analog Devices, Inc., observed that a primary purpose of his company's incentive plan, which was based on collective (either corporate or division) performance, was based on this approach:

> I do not like to refer to the plans as incentive plans. I visualize them as plans
> for communicating some important facts of life. . . . The bonus plans help
> us deliver [these facts] and enable us to share the fruits of whatever success
> we accomplish as a total organization.[22]

Provision of Necessary Resources

A final way to help employees act appropriately is simply to make sure that they have the resources they need to do a good job. The list of resources needed is highly job specific, but it might include items such as information, supplies, staff support, and/or decision aids. In larger organizations, particularly, there is a strong need for much transfer of information among organizational entities so that the coordination of effort is maintained.

PERSONNEL CONTROLS AND THE CONTROL PROBLEMS

As a group the personnel controls are capable of addressing all of the control problems, although, as shown in Table 4.1, not each type of personnel control is useful in addressing each type of problem. The lack-of-direction problem can be minimized, for example, by hiring only experienced personnel, by providing training programs, or by assigning new personnel to work groups that will

Table 4.1. Personnel Controls and the Control Problems

	Lack of Direction	Motivational Problems	Personal Limitations
Selection and placement	X	X	X
Training	X		X
Culture	X	X	
Group-based rewards	X	X	
Provision of necessary resources			X

provide good direction. The motivational problems, which may be minimal in firms with strong, beneficial cultures, can be minimized in other firms by hiring highly motivated people or by assigning people to work groups that will tend to make them adjust to group norms. Personal limitations can also be reduced through one or more types of personnel controls, particularly selection, training, and provision of necessary resources.

FEASIBILITY OF PERSONNEL CONTROLS

With just a few exceptions, feasibility is not a major constraint affecting the use of personnel controls. They are very adaptable; in fact, it is probably safe to say that all managers rely to some extent on their employees' guiding and motivating themselves. Even in a prison, with few control options available other than physical constraint and a distinct lack of goal congruence, administrators screen inmates so as not to assign dangerous personnel to high-risk jobs such as machine shop work.

Particular types of personnel controls may not be usable in some settings, however. For example, the "right" person for a job may not be available, and the available people may be considered untrainable. In addition, the organizational culture may be (typically is) very difficult to change.

CONCLUSION

This chapter has described a third major category of control alternatives — personnel controls. Managers implement personnel controls by encouraging either of two positive forces that are normally present in the organization: individual self controls and group-based social controls. These forces can be encouraged through effective personnel selection and placement, training, cultural control, group-based rewards, and provision of necessary resources.

Personnel controls have several important advantages over results controls and action controls: feasibility is generally not a serious constraint for personnel controls; their cost is often lower; and they produce fewer harmful side effects. Each of these advantages is discussed in subsequent chapters. Feasibility is the subject of Chapter 5.

NOTES

1. For example, see Anthony P. Raia, "Goal Setting and Self-Control: An Empirical Study," *Journal of Management Studies* 2 (February 1965): 34–53.
2. See, for example, Edward E. Lawler III and John G. Rhode, *Information and Control in Organizations* (Pacific Palisades, Calif.: Goodyear, 1976).
3. For example, see Kenneth J. Arrow, *The Limits of Organization* (New York: W. W. Norton, 1974).
4. For example, see Oliver E. Williamson, *Markets and Hierarchies: Analysis and Antitrust Implications* (New York: Free Press, 1975).
5. For example, see Albert O. Hirschman, *Exit, Voice and Loyalty: Responses to Decline in Firms, Organizations and States* (Cambridge, Mass.: Harvard University Press, 1970).
6. For example, see Robert L. Simons, "Control in Organizations: A Framework for Analysis," *Proceedings of the Canadian Academic Accounting Association Annual Conference,* 1982 pp. 101–13; and Vijay Sathe, "Demystifying Corporate Culture" (Working Paper no. 83–22, Graduate School of Business Administration, Harvard University, 1983).
7. For example, see James G. March and Herbert A. Simon, *Organizations* (New York: Wiley, 1958).
8. For example, see John P. Wanous, *Organizational Entry: Recruitment, Selection and Socialization of Newcomers* (Reading, Mass.: Addison-Wesley, 1980); and Richard D. Arvey, *Fairness in Selecting Employees* (Reading, Mass.: Addison-Wesley, 1979).
9. See, for example, Laura Rohmann, "Write You Are," *Forbes,* May 9, 1983, p. 185.
10. See, for example, Trudy Hayden, "Employers Who Use Lie Detector Tests," *Business and Society Review* 41 (Spring 1982): 16–21; and Susan Tompor, "More Employers Attempt to Catch a Thief by Giving Job Applicants 'Honesty' Exams," *Wall Street Journal,* August 3, 1981, p. 17.
11. "Wal-Mart: The Model Discounter," *Dun's Business Month* 120 (December 1982): 60.
12. "Jerry Reinsdorf Pulls a Double Play in Chicago," *Business Week,* October 10, 1983, p. 53.
13. Philip Selznick, *Leadership in Administration: A Sociological Interpretation* (New York: Row, Peterson, 1957).

14. Victor Faux, "Unobtrusive Controls in Organizations: An Action Research Approach to Organizational Change" (Ph.D. dissertation, Harvard University, 1981).
15. Thomas J. Peters and Robert H. Waterman, Jr., *In Search of Excellence* (New York: Harper & Row, 1982), p. 75.
16. Edgar H. Schein, "The Role of the Founder in the Creation of Organizational Culture" (Working Paper no. 1407–83, Alfred P. Sloan School of Management, Massachusetts Institute of Technology, 1983).
17. Anders Edström and Jay R. Galbraith, "Transfer of Managers as a Coordination and Control Strategy in Multinational Organizations," *Administrative Science Quarterly* 22 (June 1977): 248–63.
18. For example, see William G. Ouchi and Alfred M. Jaeger, "Type Z Organization: Stability in the Midst of Mobility," *Academy of Management Review* 3 (April 1978): 305–14.
19. Many books have been written about Japanese management practices in recent years, including their methods of influencing employee behaviors. See, for example, William G. Ouchi, *Theory Z: How American Business Can Meet the Japanese Challenge* (Reading, Mass.: Addison-Wesley, 1981); Richard T. Pascale and Anthony G. Athos, *The Art of Japanese Management* (New York: Simon & Schuster, 1981); and Rodney Clark, *The Japanese Company* (New Haven, Conn.: Yale University Press, 1979).
20. "People Power," *Forbes,* April 25, 1983, p. 170.
21. Ray J. Harris, Jr., "New Airline Surmounting Labor Dilemma," *Wall Street Journal,* September 12, 1983, p. 35.
22. Kenneth A. Merchant, "Analog Devices, Inc. (A)," case no. 9–181–001 (Boston: HBS Case Services, 1980).

chapter five

FEASIBILITY CONSTRAINTS AND THE CHOICE OF CONTROL ALTERNATIVE(S)

The preceding chapters discussed a number of devices that can be used, singly or in combinations, to accomplish good control. One of the major control decisions managers must make is which of these types of controls to use or emphasize. These control choice decisions are complex, but probably the single most significant factor affecting the choice of control(s) is *feasibility*.

This chapter provides a list of the key questions that must be addressed to determine the feasibility of the various types of controls. It also presents two brief case examples of how feasibility constraints affected — actually, largely determined — the choice of controls to be emphasized. One case describes a choice made for control of a function (bank loan officers); and the other examines a choice made for control of an entire company.

THE FEASIBILITY CONSTRAINTS IN COMBINATION

Figure 5.1 presents a summary of the questions that must be analyzed in order to make a determination of the feasibility of the control types. These questions were discussed in the earlier chapters, so only a brief overview is presented here.

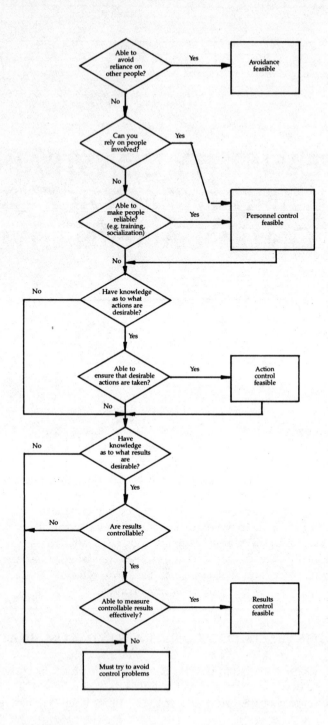

Figure 5.1. Questions to Determine Feasibility of Control Types

48

Avoidance and personnel controls are usually feasible to some extent, but they are usually not sufficient by themselves. Avoidance possibilities depend on a complex set of considerations that may be linked to corporate strategies, technologies, and management style. For example, is management willing to divest a particular activity, or subcontract the work outside? Is management able and willing to make all the critical decisions in a particular area so that authority can be centralized? Can particular individuals be replaced by, for example, automated equipment or computerized decision-making models? Avoidance strategies such as these may limit an organization's risk from exposure to control problems, but it is rarely possible to avoid all the control problems since business involves taking risks and organizations require the involvement of many people.

Similarly, personnel controls seem to be relied on to some extent in virtually all business settings, but they are rarely the final answer. Most managers are not willing to rely on the personnel controls exclusively, even after they have done all they can to encourage them.

Since avoidance and personnel controls need supplementing, the answers to the questions that determine the feasibility of results and action controls become important considerations in most situations. The feasibility of results controls depends on the answers to three questions:

1. Does knowledge exist as to what results are desirable?
2. Are the desirable results controllable by the individuals whose actions are being controlled?
3. Does the organization have the ability to measure the controllable results effectively?

Only if the answers to these three questions are all affirmative can results controls be used, and all can be limiting in many situations. Results are relatively easy to define and measure at the very top organizational levels because business organizations are usually aware of the reasons for their existence, and suitable organizationwide measures can usually be developed. At middle and lower levels, the task is much more difficult. It often takes considerable thought and much negotiation, such as during formal planning and budgeting processes, to disaggregate the total organizational objectives into result areas upon which individual lower- and middle-level participants can have some affect and for which effective measures can be developed.

The feasibility of action controls depends on the answers to two questions:

1. Does knowledge exist as to what actions are desirable?
2. Does the organization have the ability to ensure that the desirable actions are taken?

The first question is generally much more limiting than the second. It is often not possible to determine beforehand what a good action (such as, a decision) might be. The second question is generally not very limiting, as it is usually possible to ensure that desirable actions are taken through direct supervision or monitoring of action reports.

The answers to these five feasibility questions largely determine the choice of the type of control alternative, which is illustrated in the following sections in which two brief case examples are presented.

CASE 1: CONTROLLING BANK LOAN OFFICERS

In 1983 the manager of the New York branch of a large foreign bank was considering whether changes should be made in the way the account management (lending) side of the branch was controlled. The branch had grown from an initial four account managers (AMs) in 1981 to nine in 1983, and the branch manager was concerned that he was no longer able to exercise the close personal scrutiny that had kept him informed as to what the AMs were doing (action control). He was considering whether a different form of control should be emphasized.

The AMs, all of whom had previous experience at other banks, had been allowed considerable autonomy. They each had their own areas of expertise (mostly industry specializations), and they were free to identify potential clients within areas of their specialty and to conduct discussions with them as they wished within the constraints of the branch's charter. They were also allowed to make loans up to a limit of $1 million, with review by the branch loan committee only after the loans had been made.

The Present Control System and the Issue

Control was provided largely by preaction reviews, both formal and informal. Since the branch was small, it was relatively easy for the branch manager to stay well informed about the AMs' activities in order to provide informal supervision and to offer assistance that might be needed. Loan committee review of loan proposals was another part of the control system. Formal preaction reviews were required by the branch loan committee of proposals for loans greater than $1 million and by the corporate loan committee for proposals greater than $5 million. A formal report of the AMs' activities, including deals made and in progress, had been produced for a few months when the branch

Table 5.1. Feasibility of Control Alternatives for Controlling Bank Loan Officers

Question	Answer	Conclusion
I. Able to avoid reliance on other people?	No	Avoidance not feasible
II. Able to rely on other people?	Yes, but . . .	
Able to make people reliable?	No more than they are	Personnel controls feasible
III. Have knowledge as to what actions are desirable?	Yes	
Able to ensure that desirable actions are taken?	Becoming a problem	Action controls may be feasible
IV. Have knowledge as to what results are desirable?	Yes	
Are results controllable?	To some extent	
Able to measure results effectively?	No	Results controls not feasible

first opened, but the report was abandoned because the information was not being used.

The issue being discussed in 1983 was whether to replace the existing action controls with results controls. To implement the results control system, each AM would be set up as a little profit center. The AMs would be assigned an asset base and allowed to deploy it as they saw fit, within the constraints of the branch charter. They would be charged for their expenses and given credit for the profits earned, and evaluations would be based on the profits they earned for the bank.

The analysis of the feasibility of these control options is shown in Table 5.1. Avoidance of the AMs was impossible because they played a key role in the bank. Personnel controls were an important part of the control over the AMs, as all had been hired because they had good track records in their previous jobs. But the branch manager was not willing to rely completely on trust, and this was particularly true with recent hires who had had less experience. Thus, an examination of the feasibility of action and results control had to be made.

Feasibility of Action Controls

The bank managers concluded that actions controls could be made feasible. Knowledge of desirable actions was considered good. The managers judged that the most critical skill for an AM to have was the ability to manage his or her time well. The AMs were expected to spend most of their time developing significant chunks of business that could be lent at profitable rates of interest to clients that fitted with the branch's charter, and since the branch was new, the untapped market was large. A list of potential clients had been assembled and assigned priorities at branch headquarters, and it was expected that the AMs would spend most of their time working to develop the higher-priority prospects. This was the first type of desirable action.

Analysis of the loan-paying ability of customers who wanted loans was the second most important factor that determined success or failure for the AMs. The bank did not require the AMs to follow a particular analysis procedure since most of the AMs had developed their own working habits at their previous employers, but the branch manager felt that a clear difference existed between good and bad analysis and that he could recognize the differences, particularly by questioning the AMs on the details of the situation and by examining the documentation submitted as part of loan proposals.

The bank managers also saw that the ability to ensure that desirable actions were taken as potentially good, but because the branch manager was becoming increasingly unable to provide the direct supervision needed, some changes would have to be made in the way the branch was structured. Two alternatives that might be implemented to allow action controls to be continued were: (1) to add another level of supervision in the AM area, such as by promoting the most experienced AMs; or (2) to reinstitute the formal activity reports so that the branch manager could use the reports to stay abreast of the AMs' actions. Either of these options was possible; so the overall conclusion was that action controls could be continued.

Feasibility of Results Controls

The bank managers determined, on the other hand, that results controls were not feasible. Knowledge of the results desired was not the problem as it was clear that the bank wanted to earn good returns with acceptable levels of risk. But the branch's managers concluded that no good overall measure could be developed of the results that the AMs could effect. The traditional accounting profit measures were not considered to be very meaningful because, the managers felt, the true return on a loan could not be judged until the loan was finally paid off. Money that was taken as "interest income" could be dwarfed by a write-off of principal, if that ever became necessary. Thus, for the bulk of the loans, good results measures were not available until seven to ten years after the loans were made, and this was clearly not timely. No results measure that was available on a timely basis (for example, loan volume) was considered to be acceptable.

This timeliness problem would have been enough to render a total reliance on results controls infeasible, but another serious problem also existed: controllability. Results, however measured (such as, loan volume, interest income), often were poorly correlated with the effort the AMs put in. For example, some sizable loans came from referrals or existing customers, and these required little or no selling effort. Thus, for the controllability reason also, the results measures that were available were felt to be very poor indicators of the desirability of the actions taken by the AMs.

The Choice

After this diagnosis, the answer was simple. The results control option was dismissed, and management made plans to improve the action reporting system and to provide supervision for the relatively inexperienced AMs. Action controls continued to dominate the branch's control system.

CASE 2: CONTROLLING A SMALL AVIATION COMPANY

In 1971 two young MBAs with only a few years of business experience bought one of the eight fixed-base operations companies at a major Texas airport. The company was in trouble. In fiscal year 1971, it had a loss of $100,000 on sales of $2 million, and the company had a negative net worth. The new owners faced two immediate critical decisions. The first was how to conserve cash. The second, which is the focus of this discussion, was how to design the company's accounting and control system so that the operating problems that caused the financial crisis would not persist.

At the time of the purchase, the company was organized informally into six departments. The activities, and the numbers of people employed in each, were as follows: fuel (16), service and parts (8), flight training (12), avionics (1), aircraft sales (0),[1] and accounting (1). The managers of each of the departments had been with the company for some considerable length of time, but they had little formal education or knowledge of business.

The Control System and the Issue

Before the takeover the company's control system had two main elements. Local control of each of the line activities was provided by the respective department manager. Each manager provided active supervision of the personnel in the department (action control) and made the technical decisions for which they were responsible based on their many years of experience in the aviation business (personnel control).

Control of the overall company was provided by the person in accounting. She made most of the critical business decisions (for example, pricing, granting credit, buying) and was a central repository of all information; she opened all the mail and distributed information to the department managers only as she saw fit. She also managed all the receivables and payables and provided no reports of operations to the department managers. Overall, the company could have been considered to be "well controlled" only to the extent that the accounting person could be judged to have been doing a good job.

At the time of the takeover, the new owners felt that company needed a new control system. They did not want to leave the accountant in the strong central role because they wanted to run their new company themselves, and they attributed much of the blame for the company's poor performance to a poor control system.

The Feasibility Analysis

A summary of the analysis of the feasibility of the major control options is shown in Table 5.2. The analysis shows that results control was the easiest to bring into the feasible category.

Avoidance would have meant the owners' assuming the accountant's centralized role, but this was not possible. What the accountant had been doing was not documented. The new owners were not experienced in the aviation business (or any other business), and they did not feel they were capable of assuming a centralized decision-making role, at least at the time of the takeover.

Personnel control was not feasible either. The department managers had little or no management training and were not able to make the important decisions that had to be made, such as whether credit should be extended so that a sale of fuel or of an aircraft could be made. Some were not even interested in learning how to make such judgments; they were interested in aviation, not business.

Action control of the whole company was not feasible because the new owners did not know the business well enough to be able to develop decision

Table 5.2. Feasibility of Control Alternatives at a Small Aviation Company

	Question	Answer	Conclusion
I.	Able to avoid reliance on other people?	No	Avoidance not feasible
II.	Able to rely on other people?	No	Personnel controls not feasible
	Able to make people reliable?	No (in short run)	
III.	Have knowledge as to what actions are desirable?	No	Action controls not feasible
	Able to ensure that desirable actions are taken?	Not relevant	
IV.	Have knowledge as to what results are desirable?	Yes	
	Are results controllable?	Mostly yes	
	Able to measure results effectively?	Probably	Results controls could be made feasible

rules for personnel in the organization to follow. In specific parts of the company, action controls would continue to be used, however. For example, direct supervision of the fuel personnel was considered to provide adequate control.

Results control would have required delegating decision-making authority to each of the department managers and then promising rewards for accomplishment of a particular set of results. This was considered feasible because one of the new owners thought he could quickly implement an information system that would provide adequate measures of the results of each department, and he thought such a system could be used to teach the department managers to make good business decisions.

The Outcome

The new owners made the decision to emphasize results control. The organization was decentralized, and a newly designed responsibility accounting system was quickly implemented. Each department was set up as a profit center, and the department managers were given authority for all the key decisions in their areas of authority, including pricing, purchasing (subject to a purchase order limit), granting credit, and hiring. They were promised a bonus of 10 percent of their profit center's profits after an allocation of administrative costs. The owners stood by to help as necessary, and in fact they provided many hours of tutoring in business decision making.

The results were spectacular. The original results control system stayed in place for eight years. Over that time annual revenues grew to approximately $30 million, and profits grew to in excess of $1 million per year.

CONCLUSION

This chapter has provided an overview of the feasibility limitations of controls, which, it has been argued, are primary determinants of what type of control systems will (and should) be implemented. The analysis of feasibility requires addressing only a short list of questions — those shown in Figure 5.1.

If more than one type of control is feasible, the choice of controls is more complex. As will be discussed in later chapters, each form of control has some unique advantages and disadvantages. Sometimes there are advantages to using multiple forms of controls. But first it is necessary to discuss the second main control system choice: how and whether to implement the controls that are used in a tight or loose form.

NOTE

1. No people were employed in aircraft sales because the previous owner had to close the department down because he was unable to finance the inventory required by the factory. The two salespeople were laid off.

chapter six

HOW TO MAKE CONTROLS TIGHTER OR LOOSER

Many articles and books in the practitioner-oriented management literature describe firms as having "tight" controls, or as having "tightened" or "loosened" their controls, and it seems that this choice as to how tightly to apply the controls used is indeed a second major control-related decision that must be made (after the choice of controls). Oddly, the tightness aspect of control systems has received very little attention in research papers and textbooks. For example, tight and loose forms of control are discussed on less than 3 pages (out of over 700) in the most popular management control systems textbook[1] — and there only in a results-control context; and it is not mentioned at all in the other major management control textbook.[2]

It is apparent in the collection of practitioner-oriented articles that mention control system tightness that tight control can be accomplished by using any, or at least most, of the types of controls, alone or in combinations with other types of controls. It does not necessarily require detailed monthly budgets and frequent, careful reviews of performance, as described in the textbook by Robert Anthony and John Dearden,[3] although some firms have control systems with these elements that do seem to produce tight control.

The purpose of this chapter is to discuss what can be inferred about tight control from the fragments of knowledge that are available. First, it is argued that tight control is not always feasible because too little information often exists as to how the object of control relates to the overall organizational objectives. Second, where good, certain control information is available, it is argued that it is possible to make greater or less use of that information and thereby produce tighter or looser control by altering the design of the control(s) used.

TIGHT CONTROL

The benefit of any control (or control system) is derived from the increase in the likelihood that the organizational objectives will be achieved (or perhaps even exceeded) over that which could be expected if the control were not in place. This can be called *the amount of control achieved* or *the degree of certainty provided* by a control system, and it can be described in terms of how tight or loose the system is.[4] Assuming away the problems of costs and the possibilities of harmful side effects that are often coincident with tight control (these are discussed in later chapters), tight control is good because it provides a high degree of certainty that people will act as the organization wishes.

TIGHT CONTROL AS A FUNCTION OF KNOWLEDGE

One definite observation that can be made about tight control is that it is only feasible where all or most of the control problems can be avoided or, more usually, where management has detailed and reasonably certain knowledge about how one or more of the control objects — results, actions, or personnel — are related to the overall organizational objectives. This point was stated well in a recent book by Russell Stout:

> Every controlled circumstance implies a cause-effect relationship, so that a change in one causal factor will produce a predetermined change in another dependent factor. Our ability to control, therefore, is a function of our knowledge.[5]

Similarly, Anthony and Dearden observed that tight control depends on top management's having "intimate knowledge of the operations being reviewed."[6]

This seems to suggest a universal rule about control, albeit one that may be difficult to use in practice: The amount of control capable of being generated in any situation is positively related to the extent and certainty of the knowledge linking the object of control and the desired outcomes. In other words, tight control is only feasible when reasonably certain, specific knowledge is available.

Knowledge is necessary, but not sufficient, to guarantee tight control, however; that knowledge must be used. The following sections describe how each of the control types can be used to take advantage of the knowledge that is available in order to generate tight control.

TIGHT RESULTS CONTROL

The achievement of tight results control depends on the characteristics of each of the system elements: definitions of desired results, measurements of performance, and reinforcements (that is, rewards and punishments) provided.

Definition of Desired Results

Certainly if behaviors are to be directed so as to produce the results the organization desires, those result areas must be defined properly and communicated explicitly and effectively to those whose behaviors are being controlled. For control to be considered tight in a results control system, the results dimensions that are defined must be congruent with true organizational goals, specific, effectively communicated and internalized by those whose behaviors are being controlled, and complete if results control is used exclusively in a given performance area. These qualities will be discussed in turn.

Congruence

Congruence in the definition of goals is closely related to the congruence of the control measures that was discussed in Chapter 2 as being one of the prime determinants of the feasibility of results controls. Congruence failures in a results control system may result either because the true goals are not understood or defined properly or because the specific measure chosen to reflect them is not correct. Tight control means a high degree of assurance that the organization will accomplish its true goals. An incorrect understanding of what the organization's true goals are will, of course, reduce the probability that the true goals will be achieved. Thus this understanding must be considered as necessary for tight control.

For many types of organizations and for many specific areas within organizations, it is a reasonable assumption that the true goals are known; and if true, definitional congruence is not a problem. For example, it is clearly desirable for production workers to be efficient, everything else being equal. In other areas, however, goal understanding is not a reasonable assumption — as, for example, in many types of public and not-for-profit organizations[7] and in areas of corporations where goals conflict, as they often do, particularly at upper organizational levels. Then congruence becomes a more limiting problem.

Specificity

Tight results control also depends on having goals described in specific terms and in relatively short increments of time. Specific goal definitions are disaggregated and quantified: such as, $1.21 labor costs per unit, a 15 percent return on assets each quarter, and less than 1 percent customer complaints. Less specific definitions may be as vague as *do a good job, be efficient,* or *keep the customers happy.*

Gould, Inc., is an example of a company that loosened up its controls by reducing the volume and specificity of the information used to monitor its divisions. Previously, division managers had to submit a weekly budget containing 12 pieces of information including daily sales, order backlog, and working capital — not just a "bottom-line" number;[8] but in January 1983 Gould top management made a concerted effort to loosen up its controls by reviewing performance only monthly and allowing division managers to operate more autonomously.[9] Why did they loosen the control? It was done in order to minimize some negative side effects of the tight controls, particularly the creation of unacceptable operating delays and discouragement of innovation. (These are discussed in Chapter 7.)

Results standards, of course, may be derived from any of a number of sources including engineering studies, historical performance, or comparisons with competitors. In some areas of most companies, detailed and specific standards are not feasible; it is usually difficult to be specific as to how many cases a lawyer should handle in a year, for example, or what is meant by *ethical behavior,* but specificity is one of the elements necessary for the implementation of tight results control.

Communication and Internalization

It is obvious that for results control to be tight, goals must be communicated effectively and internalized by those charged with their accomplishment, as only then can they have significance for performance. The degree to which goals are understood and internalized seems to be affected by many factors, including the qualifications of the personnel involved, the amount of participation allowed in the goal-setting processes, the perceived degree of controllability, and the reasonableness of the goals. Internalization is likely to be low, for example, where goals are too tight, where the results are not considered controllable, or, perhaps, where those whose behaviors are being controlled are not allowed to participate in setting the goals.

Failure to obtain internalization of goals can cause problems, as William Hartman found when he took over Interpace Corporation, a $350 million (sales) conglomerate in Parsippany, New Jersey. Hartman attempted to transform Interpace into a dynamic growth company in part by implementing an ITT-type control system built around focusing on financial results and "compelling managers to abide by financial dicta." The results, however, were poor, apparently because the managers never understood either their goals or how they were to accomplish them. The managers claimed that Hartman "kept his strategic goals to himself." Hartman claims he was consistently "frustrated [because] people don't see the important factors in getting to goal."[10]

Completeness

A final requirement for tight results control, which is only important if results controls are used exclusively, or at least extensively, is completeness. Completeness means that the result areas defined in the control system include all the areas in which the organization desires good performance and for which the individual involved can have some impact. When goal specifications are incomplete, individuals often allow areas not in their goal set to slip.[11] For example, a purchasing manager who is evaluated solely on meeting cost standards may allow quality to slip, and salesmen who are asked to meet a sales volume quota are likely to strive for volume, at the expense, possibly, of smaller but more profitable sales.

In a hybrid control system made up of some combination of results, actions, and personnel controls, the definition of results areas does not have to be complete. But some care must certainly be taken to ensure that all significant potential control problems are covered in some manner.

Measurement of Performance

Tight results control also depends on the effectiveness of the measures of performance that are generated. As discussed in earlier chapters, results control relies on measures that are congruent, precise, objective, timely, and understandable; a control system that is used to apply tight control requires excellence in all of these measurement qualities. If tight control is attempted while measurement fails on any of these qualities, harmful side effects are almost inevitable. Some of these are discussed in the following chapter.

Rewards or Punishments

Tight results control also depends on having rewards and punishments that are directly linked to the accomplishment (or nonaccomplishment) of the desired results and that are significant to the individuals involved. Unfortunately, the strength of the effects of any reward system reinforcement is often difficult to predict, as it is clear from much research that different individuals often react differently to identical rewards or punishments.[12]

Rewards need not be monetary, of course; many employees respond to other rewards such as job security, recognition, or self-satisfaction. Several studies have shown that the desired control effects may even result from merely reporting measures of performance, with no rewards provided explicitly[13] — the reports provide useful information and the people involved want to do well.

At General Mills, Inc., entrepreneurs whose companies have been acquired but who stay on as division managers are motivated with sizable performance bonuses. But bonuses and threat of divestment seem to provide less motivation than does the desire to avoid embarrassment before their peers. As one such entrepreneur, Thad Eure, Jr., president of the Darryl's Restaurant chain acquired by General Mills in 1980, noted: "Our pride makes us want to show these people what we can do."[14]

Results-related reinforcement appears to be very weak at top management levels in most companies. Monetary rewards for top managers often have little or no relationship to company performance. It is natural that most managers, being risk averse, would rather receive guaranteed payments (that is, salary) rather than payments that are contingent on performance. But many companies have been criticized for allowing this to happen; several recent articles have noted that "many compensation committees [of boards of directors] are rubber stamps, unwilling to be hard-nosed about the pay of top executives."[15] The recent trend in management compensation, however, is toward strengthening the link between compensation and performance.[16]

An Example

Control of drivers at United Parcel Service (UPS) of America, Inc. is a good example of use of tight results control. UPS pays good wages but pushes its drivers hard. Management compares each driver's performance (how many miles, how many deliveries, how many pickups) every day with a computerized projection of what performance should have been. Drivers who cannot meet the standards are assigned a supervisor to ride with them to provide suggestions for improvement, and those who do not improve can be warned, suspended, and eventually dismissed.[17]

This control system meets every characteristic of tight results control. The goals seem to be congruent because the company has been very successful; it dominates the small-package delivery market. They seem to be complete, as a driver has no other significant responsibilities other than to deliver packages efficiently. The goals are very specific; measurement is thorough and done on a very frequent (that is, daily) basis; and the rewards, which include job security and sizable amounts of money, are significant to the personnel involved.

TIGHT ACTION CONTROLS

Action controls come in more forms than do results control systems. Since the forms of action control are quite different from one another, the ways in which each might be used to achieve tight control must be discussed separately.

Behavioral Constraints

Tight control in some areas of a company can be provided by behavioral constraints, both physical and administrative. Physical constraints come in many forms, ranging from simple locks on desks to elaborate software and electronic security systems. No simple rules can be provided as to the degree of control they provide except, perhaps, that extra protection usually costs more. But the controls used in most bank vault areas are a good example of a control system that is tight, largely owing to the physical constraints used.

Administrative constraints also provide widely varying degrees of control. Centralizing more of the key decisions provides tighter control (1) if it can be assumed that upper-level managers can be expected to make more reliable decisions and (2) if it can be guaranteed that those who do not have authority for certain actions cannot violate the constraints that have been established. And separating sensitive duties among a larger number of people should make the accomplishment of a forbidden task less likely; therefore, control can be described as tighter.

Preaction Reviews

By themselves, preaction reviews sometimes cause control systems, both in a specific area and in an entire company, to be considered tight if the reviews are frequent, detailed, and performed by a knowledgeable person (or persons). Tight preaction reviews often include thorough scrutiny of all business plans by staff personnel and multiple levels of managers, including top management. They can also include examination of proposals for expenditures of even small money amounts before approvals are given.

Examples of tight preaction reviews abound. At Irving Oil, Ltd., a company that operates 3,000 gas stations throughout Eastern Canada, control is considered tight, as Irving personnel "don't buy pencils before checking with [the chairman]."[18] At most banks control is usually exercised more tightly over foreign branches than domestic branches; domestic branch managers are more frequently given the power to sign for larger loans without headquarter's approval. And as mentioned earlier, it is preaction reviews that give Amerada Hess its reputation of having a tight control system — the chairman "pursues his business down to its grimiest details."[19]

Action Accountability

The amount of control generated by an action accountability control system depends on the same types of factors that were discussed as affecting the amount of control generated by a results control system: the definitions of desirable and undesirable actions, the effectiveness of the action-tracking system, and the reinforcement provided.

Definitions of Actions

As with results controls, the definitions of actions in an action accountability control system must be congruent, specific, well communicated, and complete. *Congruence* means that the performance (or nonperformance) of the actions defined in the control system will indeed lead to the achievement of the true organizational goals. Clearly, for control to be tight — meaning a high probability of achievement of the true goals — the definition of desirable actions must be congruent.

Tighter control can also be effected by making the definitions of acceptability more specific. *Specificity* means defining the desirable behaviors in the form of work rules (for example, no smoking) or specific policies (such as, a purchasing policy to obtain three competing bids before releasing a purchase order), as opposed to general guidelines or vague codes of conduct (for example, act professionally).

Understanding and *acceptance,* on the part of those whose behaviors are being controlled is essential. If the people involved do not understand the rules, they cannot be affected by them; and if they do not accept them, they may try to find ways to avoid the system. Understanding and acceptance can be improved through developing effective communication processes and, perhaps, by allowing participation in the rule-defining processes.

Finally, *completeness* is important. This means that all the important, acceptable actions are well defined. Completeness is especially important if action accountability controls are relied on exclusively or extensively.

Effectiveness of Action Tracking

Control in an action accountability control system can also be made tighter by improving the effectiveness of the action-tracking system. Personnel who are certain that their actions will be noticed, and relatively quickly, will be affected more strongly by an action accountability control system than will those who feel that the chance of their being observed is small. Constant direct supervision is one tight action-tracking method. Detailed audits of action reports is another. This type of tight control apparently takes place at Commodore International, as the chairman, Jack Tramiel, is said to provide detailed reviews of expenses, sometimes down to items costing as little as $25.[20]

Rewards or Punishments

Finally, control can be made tighter by making the rewards or punishments more significant to the individuals affected. In general, this impact should vary directly with the size of the reward (or the severity of the punishment), although different individuals may react differently to identical rewards or punishments.

An Example

Control of commercial pilots is a good example of very tightly applied action accountability control system. Pilots are given very detailed checklists of nearly all required actions, not only for normal operations but also for all foreseeable contingencies (such as, engine failure, fire on board, hijacking). Intensive training helps ensure that the procedures are understood, and frequent checking and updating helps ensure that they remain in the pilot's active memory. The tracking of deviant actions is precise and timely as all potential violations are thoroughly screened by objective investigators. Finally, reinforcement is significant because severe penalties, including loss of profession (and loss of life), are threatened.

TIGHT PERSONNEL CONTROLS

The degree of control provided by the personnel controls is very difficult to assess. In voluntary organizations, personnel controls usually provide a significant amount of control, as most volunteers derive a keen sense of satisfaction just from doing a good job, however that is defined to them, and they will thus be motivated to do well. This can also be the case in some business situations — such as small family-run businesses — where the already-present, individual personnel controls may be totally effective because of the complete, or at least extensive, overlap between the desires of the organization and those of the individuals on whom it must rely. But in most business organizations, the natural overlap between individual and organizational objectives is not only smaller, it is unstable, and the impending divergence between the objectives is very difficult to observe.

The effectiveness of the steps that might be taken to increase the strength of the personnel controls is also very difficult to assess. In general, it is a function of the knowledge available to link the control mechanism with the solution of the existing control problems; but often the information about how well factors such as education, experience, and personality predict performance is not reliable.

Cultural controls, however, can sometimes be very powerful and stable. Culture involves a set of shared beliefs and values that employees use to guide behavior. Some companies' cultures can be termed *strong* because they include quite a few deeply held and widely shared beliefs and values. IBM, Electronic Data Systems, Hewlett-Packard, Johnson & Johnson, and Procter & Gamble are companies that are usually considered to have a strong culture.[21] Most large companies, have weak cultures, however, because of their diversity and dispersion of people.

It is probably safe to say that with the exception of companies with strong cultures, tight control probably cannot be effected with the use of these devices alone. Most personnel controls are unstable. They can break down very quickly if demands, opportunities, or needs change, and they provide little or no warning of failure.

CONCLUSION

This chapter has focused on another major characteristic of controls and control systems about which managers must make decisions: their degrees of tightness. Although there is a negative connotation associated with the use of the term, it has been argued here that *tight control* — defined as meaning a high degree of assurance that people will behave as the organization wishes — is good. With this definition in mind, it seems clear that when managers in an organization have good knowledge about what should be done, they should implement tight controls, using any of the designs discussed in this chapter. This is true, however, only if it can be assumed that the harmful side effects that often accompany tight control can be avoided or minimized. It is these side effects that have caused the negative connotation associated with the term tight control.

With the usual exception of personnel controls, all of the control types can be used to provide tight or loose control, depending on how and where they are designed and used. A summary of the characteristics of each of the control types that can be varied to produce tighter or looser control is presented in Table 6.1.

Table 6.1. Tightness of Control and Design of Controls Used

Type of Control	What Makes It Tight
Results or action accountability	Definition of desired results or actions: Congruent with true organizational goals Specific Effectively communicated and internalized Complete (if accountability emphasized) Measurement of results or tracking of actions: Congruent Precise Objective Timely Understandable Rewards or punishments: Significant to person(s) involved
Behavioral constraints	More restrictive
Preaction reviews	Frequent Detailed Performed by informed person(s)
Personnel controls	Certainty and stability of knowledge linking personnel characteristics with desired actions

Managers are not limited to tinkering with the characteristics of just one form of control, of course. There are many examples of situations where a particular type of control has been replaced with another type, which provides a better fit with the situation, in order to tighten controls. For example, management at Varian Associates, Inc., was considered to have tightened up its controls because they replaced the company's "gentlemanly 'atta boy' approach" (personnel control) with results controls, which included division-level incentive plans for improved financial performance and strict targets for inventory and receivables levels.[22] Alternatively, top management of Texas Instruments tightened up controls over the company's troubled consumer electronics areas by deemphasizing results controls and emphasizing detailed preaction reviews.[23]

Managers do not have to rely exclusively on a single type of control; they can also effect tighter control by implementing multiple forms of controls. For example, control over the line personnel in casinos (for example, dealers) must be considered tight because casinos have (1) strict licensing requirements (personnel control); (2) multiple forms of direct scrutiny of behaviors — including up to three levels of direct supervision, use of closed circuit cameras, and observation through one-way mirrors (the so-called eye-in-the-sky) — (action control); and (3) detailed requirements for paperwork so that good audit trails are created to document transfers of cash and cash equivalents (action control).

The Continental Illinois National Bank & Trust can be used as another example. Management at the bank tightened up controls by insisting on more extensive loan documentation, which was to be reviewed and approved by more bank officers than required previously before a loan was authorized (preaction review). At the same time, they created a new credit-review division to analyze the loan portfolio in a more careful, more objective, more timely fashion (results control).[24]

Tight control of even relatively small problems may require the implementation of multiple forms of control. For example, a recent article discussed how to control the proliferation of forms within an organization.[25] The recommendation was to limit responsibility for designing new forms to just a few individuals (behavioral constraint) and to establish procedures to guide decisions as to when a new form is warranted and what they should look like (action control).

These are typical examples. When they wish to implement tight controls or to tighten up the existing controls, most managers use more than one type of control — in effect, overlapping controls. They rely on, for example, selecting good people, establishing some formal procedures, implementing some accountability for results, and reviewing some key decisions before they are made.

At the corporate level, tight control almost always involves multiple forms of control. Under Harold Geneen, ITT was considered to have a proto-typical tight control system. The company hired good managers and moti-vated them by paying large results-dependent bonuses that brought their total salaries to approximately 30 percent over comparable jobs in other firms. A very detailed planning, budgeting, and reporting system was in place, and top management used it to monitor the plans and activities of all business units. A large staff organization was used to monitor the line managers' activities and performances. It is significant, however, that much of the tight control infra-structure at ITT has been dismantled under the new chief executive, Rand Ar-askog, in part because it did not suit his managerial style. But a perhaps more important reason was that Araskog had serious concern that he might be lack-ing the knowledge necessary to implement tight controls.[26]

The knowledge required to implement tight controls is, unfortunately, often not present, and if tight controls are attempted in the absence of this knowledge, many harmful side effects are possible. It is these side effects that are most responsible for the many negative feelings that are often associated with the mere mention of tight control. The most significant harmful side ef-fects and their causes and possible solutions are discussed in the next two chap-ters.

NOTES

1. Robert N. Anthony and John Dearden, *Management Control Systems* (Homewood, Ill.: Richard D. Irwin, 1980), pp. 459–61.
2. Jerry Dermer, *Management Planning and Control Systems* (Homewood, Ill.: Richard D. Irwin, 1977).
3. Anthony and Dearden, *Management Control Systems*.
4. This is a broad conceptualization of the terms. *Tight control* is sometimes used in a narrower sense to mean "allowing only limited autonomy."
5. Russell Stout, Jr., *Management or Control?: The Organizational Challenge* (Blooming-ton: Indiana University Press, 1980), p. 4.
6. Anthony and Dearden, *Management Control Systems*, p. 459.
7. Geert H. Hofstede, "Management Control of Public and Not-for-Profit Activities," *Accounting, Organizations and Society* 6 (1981): 1193–216.
8. "The Controller: Inflation Gives Him More Clout with Management," *Business Week*, August 15, 1977, p. 87.
9. Heywood Klein, "Gould Loosens Up as It Gains in High-Tech, But Some Doubt Strong Chief Will Let Go," *Wall Street Journal*, May 26, 1983, p. 33.
10. "How a Winning Formula Can Fail," *Business Week*, May 25, 1981, pp. 119–20.
11. This observation has been made by many authors. For example, see Edward E. Lawler III and John G. Rhode, *Information and Control in Organizations* (Pacific Pali-

sades, Calif.: Goodyear, 1976); and John G. Rhode and Fulton M. Smith, Jr., "Cost Accounting and Organizational Behavior," in *The Managerial and Cost Accountant's Handbook,* ed. Homer A. Black and James D. Edwards (Homewood, Ill.: Dow Jones–Irwin, 1979), pp. 257–94.

12. Edward E. Lawler III, *Pay and Organization Development* (Reading, Mass.: Addison-Wesley, 1980).

13. See, for example, Prem Prakash and Alfred Rappaport, "Informational Interdependencies: System Structure Induced by Accounting Information," *Accounting Review* (October 1975): 723–34; and Regina Herzlinger and Frederic Hooper, "The Impact of Financial Information: An Empirical Study of Professionals in a Nonprofit Organization" (Working Paper, Graduate School of Business Administration, Harvard University, March 1983).

14. "How to Manage Entrepreneurs," *Business Week,* September 7, 1981, p. 69.

15. For example, see Carol J. Loomis, "The Madness of Executive Compensation," *Fortune,* July 12, 1982, p. 45.

16. For example, see E. S. Mruk and J. A. Giardino, "Executive Compensation: Eleventh Edition Study," *Financial Executive* L (October 1983): 42–50; and "Executive Compensation: Looking to the Long Term Again," *Business Week,* May 9, 1983, pp. 80–83.

17. "Behind the UPS Mystique: Puritanism and Productivity," *Business Week,* June 6, 1983, pp. 66–73.

18. Alan Freeman and John Urquart, "Hard-Working Irvings Maintain Tight Control in a Canadian Province," *Wall Street Journal,* November 1, 1983, p. 1.

19. Steve Mufson, "Amerada Hess Chief Keeps Controls Tight, Emphasizes Marketing," *Wall Street Journal,* January 11, 1983, p. 1.

20. Susan Chace and Michael W. Miller, "Commodore's Tramiel Sharpens Competition in Small Computers," *Wall Street Journal,* August 18, 1983, p. 1.

21. For example, Thomas J. Peters and Robert H. Waterman, Jr., *In Search of Excellence* (New York: Harper & Row, 1982); "Demystifying Corporate Culture" (Working Paper no. 83–22, Graduate School of Business Administration, Harvard University, 1983); and Robert E. Lee, "How H. Ross Perot Builds Fierce Loyalty at EDS in Dallas," *International Management* 38 (March 1983): 33.

22. Kathleen K. Wiegner, "It's About Time," *Forbes,* April 25, 1983, pp. 41–42.

23. See, for example, David Stipp, "Texas Instruments Seeks Comeback Trail in Consumer Electronics; Outlook Is Hazy," *Wall Street Journal,* September 12, 1983, p. 4.

24. John Helyar, "Big Continental Illinois Hopes It Will Recover as U.S. Economy Does," *Wall Street Journal,* January 5, 1983, p. 1.

25. See W. Koeneke, "Forms Control — Fortune or Flop?," *Journal of Systems Management* 32 (January 1981): 11–14.

26. "ITT: Groping for a New Strategy," *Business Week,* December 15, 1980, pp. 66–80.

chapter seven

THE POTENTIAL FOR HARMFUL SIDE EFFECTS

The harmful side effects that controls can bring about loom as a very important consideration for those who are designing and implementing controls. Some of these side effects are inherent in the use of specific types of controls, but despite their presence, they are often considered not serious enough to warrant the avoidance or abandonment of the control type. Other harmful side effects are avoidable; they are caused either by poor design, by implementation of the wrong type of control for the given situation, or both. Where side effects exist, the tighter the controls are applied, usually the more severe the side effects. Thus, managers must understand what these side effects are and what causes them so that they can avoid the most harmful problems and make informed judgments as to the risks and total costs of using particular types of controls.

This chapter provides an overview of what is known about some of the major negative side effects produced by one or more of the control types. These include: (1) behavioral displacement, (2) gamesmanship, (3) operating delays, and (4) negative attitudes. Chapter 8 focuses in more detail on the problems caused by the use of financial controls, the form of results control that involves holding individuals, particularly general managers, accountable for results defined in monetary terms.

BEHAVIORAL DISPLACEMENT

Behavioral displacement is one of the most common and most harmful control system side effects. It occurs wherever the behaviors encouraged by the control system are not consistent with the organization's objectives, or at least the strategy that has been selected.

Displacement has several causes. It is most common with accountability-type controls (either results or action accountability) where the specification of results or actions desired is incongruent or incomplete, but it also results at times from the use of social controls. These three situations are discussed in the following sections.

Displacement and Results Controls

A very common and serious failure of results-oriented control systems is caused by the definition of goal sets that are incongruent. Steven Kerr[1] described this problem as "the folly of rewarding A while hoping for B." Martin Landau and Russell Stout[2] called it a "Type II error" of control systems because it is similar to the case in statistics where an hypothesis is accepted as true when it is actually false; in their analogy, the null hypothesis is that the set of goals used in the results control system is an accurate representation of the true organizational goals.

Examples of failures to define goals congruently abound. For example, Chris Argyris[3] and Peter Blau[4] both described situations where monthly quotas were used at the core of results control systems with displacement effects. In both situations the employees selected the easiest jobs, not those that had the highest priority or that were the most profitable, in order to meet their quotas.

John Kotter, Leonard Schlesinger, and Vijay Sathe described an example of displacement in a corporate research laboratory that implemented a results control system with the number of patents filed as an indicator of research effectiveness.[5] The effect was an increase in the number of patents filed but a decrease in the number of successful research projects.

The displacement occurring in situations such as these where results control incongruencies exist seems to be caused by one or both of two major factors: a poor understanding of the desired results and/or an overreliance on easily quantified results.

Poor Understanding of Desired Results

The first major cause of displacement is an incorrect or incomplete understanding of the role of the person(s) being controlled. An incorrect understanding of what needs to be done might occur in a company that sets sales quotas for its "cash-cow" departments based on volume, not profitability. Volume-based quotas might be appropriate for a department in an industry with manufacturing costs declining with experience, but in a stable, cash-generating business, such targets are likely to reflect merely an imperfect understanding of the appropriate strategy.

Results control can also cause displacement if there is an incomplete specification of the results that are desired. In these cases even conscientious individuals will be induced to concentrate their energy on the results or actions monitored by the control system and to slight other important actions. In other words it becomes possible to maximize performance according to the rules of the control system without concurrently contributing optimally toward the organization's objectives. The following examples illustrate the point:

- A plant manager was unwilling to modify production schedules to accommodate rush orders that could be large and very profitable. Because he was evaluated as a cost center, not as a profit center, he had little incentive to make last-minute schedule changes.[6]
- A community health center began to report the costs of providing each type of service (such as, physical exam, walk-in visit) by each medical practitioner involved in order to supplement the practitioners' dedication to patients with a greater concern for costs. The effect was dramatic — unit costs declined sharply — but efficiency did not seem to be affected, as very little of the cost decline was due to a reduction in the time per encounter. What did happen was that the practitioners saw more patients and therefore spent more of their time in direct patient care. This was, however, at the expense of other objectives of the health center, such as the furtherance of community health-maintenance programs and training of community nonprofessionals.[7]
- A trailer company decided to monitor the number of trailers their salespeople sold. The result was indeed a dramatic improvement in sales, but many of the sales were to poor credit risks, and the sales lot quickly filled up with overpriced trade-ins.[8]
- A department store implemented a results control system that involved rewarding sales personnel on the volume of sales they generated. Just after the introduction of the control system, sales did increase, but this turned out to be only a short-term improvement. As the sales personnel learned how to maximize their performance according to the rules of the control system, they began to compete among themselves for customers and to neglect important activities for which they were not rewarded, such as stocking and arrangement of merchandise.[9]

As these situations illustrate, relying on results control with an incomplete specification of desired results can be costly. A complete understanding of the trade-offs required of a person in the role being controlled is particularly important when multiple indicators are used to monitor different aspects of performance because a method of aggregation must be set so that the individual measures can be combined into an overall performance measure. If the relative importance of the various factors is not made explicit, employees may not allocate their effort appropriately, and the outcome will not be optimal.[10] .

Similarly, incorrect or incomplete sets of goals have been blamed as one of the causes for the common lack of success of MBO systems. Here is an example of such a criticism:

> Tying personnel performance evaluation, promotions, compensation and the like to objective-achievement is often counterproductive, because it discourages the development of innovative, high-risk, high-reward objectives.[11]

Overquantification

A second major cause of displacement in results control systems is a common tendency "to concentrate on matters that are concrete and quantifiable, rather than intangible concepts" that may be even more important.[12] Peter Drucker has been among those who have commented on this problem:

> The more we can quantify the truly measurable areas, the greater the temptation to put all-out on those — the greater, therefore, the danger that what looks like better "controls" will actually mean less "control" if not a business out of control altogether.[13]

This type of criticism was recently leveled at Mattel, Inc., the toy company that moved into consumer electronics. An independent observer criticized the company as being "a highly structured, run-by-the-numbers type of company in a business that requires more intuitive management."[14]

Avoiding quantified indicators is not the general solution to these criticisms, because quantified indicators are not inherently bad and they do have some advantages, particularly with regard to the clarity with which goals and results can be communicated. One solution to the results controls–related displacement problem is to find or to develop acceptable quantified indicators of the intangible concepts that may be missing in order to alleviate the problems for which results controls are being criticized. For example, an acceptable surrogate measure of quality might be "percent rejects," and employee welfare might be assessed by means of attitude surveys.

However, situations do exist where quantified measures cannot be used; for example, it may not be possible to develop timely measures of success for research scientists. And there does seem to be an ever-present risk that quantified measures will be overused (that is, used where they do not provide an acceptably close representation of the actual quality desired).

Displacement and Action Controls

Displacement can also occur where action controls are used. This is sometimes known as *means-ends inversion* because employees can be induced to pay more attention to what they do (the means) and can lose sight of what they are to accomplish (the ends).

Many instances of displacement are due to incongruent action sets. Incongruence occurs wherever performance of the specified actions would not be the most desirable from the organization's standpoint, in the sense that optimal results could not be expected if those actions were performed. For example, Peter Drucker observed that

> a company that tells its foremen that the job is human relations but which promotes the foreman who best does his paper work makes it very clear to even the dumbest man in the shop that it wants paper work rather than human relations. And it will get paper work.[15]

Peter Blau[16] described a good example of a displacement problem produced in an action accountability control system. He observed a public employment agency that controlled its interviewers by monitoring the number of interviews conducted. This caused a goal displacement problem because the interviewers were motivated to increase the number of interviews they conducted, but they were not spending enough time actually locating jobs for their clients. Eventually, the agency recognized the displacement problem, and agency management started to control both actions and results. They devised eight quantitative measures (for example, number of placements, number of referrals, ratios of placements to interviews and placements to referrals) and monitored them to control the performances of the interviewers.

The creation of rigid, nonadaptive behaviors is another form of displacement that often occurs where action controls are used. It is a pathology commonly associated with bureaucratic forms of organization. In their struggle to survive and prosper, all organizations must deal with changing, uncertain environments, albeit to different degrees, and formal action controls — for example, in the form of standard operating procedures and rules — can cause employees to routinize their behaviors and discourage them from thinking about how they might do their jobs better and adapt to a possibly changing environment. In other words, standardized operating procedures and rules tend to filter away environmental inconsistencies and to encourage a complacency to environmental change. This problem was noted by Adam Smith even before the rise of the modern corporation:

> The man whose whole life is spent in performing a few simple operations . . . has no occasion to exert his understanding or to exercise his invention. . . . He generally becomes as stupid and ignorant as it is possible for a human creature to become.[17]

More recently, Daniel Katz and Robert Kahn called procedural control systems "maintaining systems" because they serve to perpetuate the status quo.[18] Michael McCaskey observed that unless there is absolute certainty about what needs to be done, people should "avoid too narrow a focus which would reduce the chances of seeing a new combination of ideas."[19] And Stephen Robert, chief executive at Oppenheimer & Co., a large stock brokerage house, noted that "unless you reward people as entrepreneurs, they become technocrats."[20]

Examples of control system-caused rigid behaviors abound. A widely publicized example took place at IBM Corporation. After the company suffered well-publicized production and cost problems with its System 360 computer, Thomas Watson ordered the institution of an elaborate system of checks and balances in new-product testing. The effect of the controls was, however, to make the IBM people so cautious that they stopped taking risks. When Frank Cary became president of IBM, one of the first things he did was to loosen the controls because

> he recognized that the new system would indeed prevent such an expensive problem from ever happening again, but its rigidity would also keep IBM from ever developing another major system.[21]

This is a displacement problem because if the control system were designed to force individuals to think about survivability and long-term consequences, adaptability would be on their minds constantly.

Similarly, tight action controls caused problems at Gulf & Western Industries' (G&W) at G & W's Consolidated Cigar, Inc. division. Alexander N. Brainard, Consolidated's president, observed that G&W's dislike of any action that deviated from plans "stifled creativity."[22] In March 1982 Brainard and other Consolidated managers took the company private. They immediately loosened controls over personnel such as salesmen, and in Brainard's words, "we haven't had growth like this in my 13 years with Consolidated."[23]

Thus, while formal action control systems, which usually include elaborate repertoires of standard operating procedures and detailed plans, tend to make the behavior of individuals in the firm more consistent, they often make it difficult for those individuals to adapt to, and sometimes even to see, changing circumstances. This is the battle being faced at Campbell Soup Company, a company that is in the process of giving its managers more autonomy. As a Campbell manager noted:

> If all your life you worked for people who told you when to step and where to step, you don't quite know how to take it when suddenly somebody says, "Go to it, you're on your own."[24]

The conclusion, then, is that action controls and bureaucratization can be good in stable environments because they help establish good, efficient work habits; but in changing environments, they become very dangerous, even to the point where they can threaten the survival of the firm.

Displacement and Personnel Controls

Displacement is less a problem with personnel controls, but it can exist if, for example, the company is recruiting the wrong type of person for a job. Relying on social control can also cause displacement in some cases because the standards that the groups use to guide the behaviors of the group members may not be totally in line with what the organization desires. For example, many organizations rely on the fact that research scientists are highly professional and will control themselves better than the organization could by implementing formal controls. To a large extent, this is probably true, but many research scientists are motivated to acquire patents and write papers in areas that have little or no immediate commercial applications for their firm because they get a sense of personal accomplishment and a furtherance of their reputations. Doctors, too, are highly motivated by their professional standards to provide good health care, but sometimes they have little concern for financial considerations (until they establish their own practices). These are clear examples of displacement caused by a reliance on social controls.

Social controls also tend to reduce an organization's ability to adapt to a changing environment. Groups tend to induce conformity to group norms, and this may stifle creative approaches to organizational problems.

Solutions to the Displacement Problems

The key to solving, or at least alleviating, displacement problems is recognizing the problems and diagnosing the causes. This means studying to see if there is a difference between what employees are supposed to do and what the control system motivates them to do. Then if a displacement problem is deemed to exist, many solutions can usually be considered.

For example, in the department store example described above, where the sales personnel neglected their stocking and merchandise-arrangement duties, the managers might have simply rewarded their personnel for maintaining well-stocked and neatly arranged departments. Alternatively, they might have been able to redefine the areas of responsibility (the organization structure) so that the sales areas were completely independent, and the employees would then have seen that it was to their own advantage to perform the necessary maintenance activities. A third possibility might have been to supplement the results-oriented controls with other types of controls. Action controls, such as in the form of work rules or direct supervision, could have been used to ensure that the stocking and arranging was performed; or personnel controls, such as in the form of training, could have been used to help the salespeople understand the need to keep the racks stocked and properly arranged.

Displacement is one of the most serious negative control system side effects. It is very difficult to avoid the problems of completeness and congruence; it is so difficult in fact that it has led some to suggest that it is not worth trying to develop results control systems in many situations.[25] But there is no question but that results control systems can be used to influence behavior in a wide range of situations, and one of the basic assumptions about controls that most managers (at least those in the U.S.) have is that "if we want managers [or other individuals] to do something different, we should pay them for doing something different."[26] Managers must always be aware of the potential for goal displacement, however, as it is a serious and pervasive problem that is not always easy to detect.

GAMESMANSHIP

The term *gamesmanship* is used here to refer generally to the actions that managers take that are intended to improve their measures of performance without producing any positive economic effects. Gamesmanship is a particularly acute problem with accountability forms of control — either results or actions accountability — as efforts to influence either the targets or the measures that make up these systems are relatively common. Two major forms of gamesmanship, creation of slack and data manipulation, are discussed below.

Creation of Slack Resources

Slack involves consumption of assets by organizational members in excess of what is required.[27] It involves tactical responses by individuals who are motivated to keep the control system from hurting them, and it has potentially severe dysfunctional effects.

The research evidence that has been gathered suggests that significant amounts of slack do exist in most business organizations. The conclusion of one detailed study of three divisions of three separate *Fortune* 500 firms was that slack might be as much as 20 to 25 percent of the divisions' budgeted operating expenses.[28] Another study conducted in five firms found that 80 percent of the managers interviewed were willing to admit that they bargained for slack.[29]

Slack has some beneficial and some negative effects. On the positive side, slack can reduce manager tension[30] and increase organizational resiliency to change.[31] On the negative side, it can cause an inefficient allocation of resources and, consequently, inferior operating performance. Another dysfunctional effect of slack is information distortion. Slack adds a "pathology"[32] to the information set, which can make it difficult to separate the true, underlying operating performance from the consumption of excess resources.

In most situations, slack is nearly impossible to prevent. Theoretically, slack is feasible only where superiors have less-than-complete knowledge about what can be accomplished in any given area and/or where measurement of results fails to satisfy the precision criterion; so where it is possible to set tight and accurate standards and to develop precise measures of performance, it should be possible to detect slack easily. Unfortunately, however, those conditions exist only in very stable, structured situations, and if accountability controls are used in other situations, slack must be considered to be almost inevitable.

Data Manipulation

Data manipulation is another form of gamesmanship that is a common side effect of accountability-type control systems. Manipulation involves an effort on the part of the individual being controlled to "look good" by fudging the control indicators, and it comes in two basic forms: *falsification* and *smoothing*.[33] Falsification simply involves reporting erroneous data. Smoothing involves affecting the time period in which a control indicator (that is, a report of either a result or an action) appears. This might be done either to delay the appearance of an unfavorable indicator, perhaps in hopes that it can be corrected by good performance in subsequent periods, or just to obscure a trend line. Smoothing can be accomplished in several ways: by reporting facts selectively, by choosing an appropriate measurement method (such as, an accounting change), or by affecting estimates of future uncertain events (such as, allowance for uncollectable loans).

The evidence available suggests that data manipulation is very common. For example, a survey was recently conducted of general managers in a large diversified corporation that is generally highly regarded for its management excellence. In the survey 46 percent of the managers admitted that they shifted funds between accounts to avoid budget overruns.[34]

Similar evidence about other managers is constantly being uncovered. Recently, managers in a number of major U.S. corporations — including Union Carbide, Chrysler, Firestone Tire & Rubber Co., and H. J. Heinz Co. — have been observed trying to boost earnings by adopting "liberal" accounting methods, and it has been observed that "a primary factor behind many companies' fancy financial footwork . . . is incentive plans and stock options."[35] While perfectly legal, these measurement-method changes were apparently motivated to improve the indications of performance, as defined in the control system, even though "real" economic performance had not improved.

Some of the manipulation attempts are more insidious and involve outright fraud. A recent case in the Datapoint Corporation shows evidence of both falsification and smoothing. In Datapoint, marketing employees were alleged to have performed a number of questionable activities, including shipping products to customers who had not yet passed credit checks, using Datapoint's money to pay warehousing fees for distributors who would not accept shipments for which they did not have room, and shipping products to at least one fictitious customer, just to get products out the door before a quarter ended.[36]

Another recent example occurred in the grocery products division of McCormick & Co. Employees allegedly improperly delayed recording payments and expenses, altered invoices, improperly recorded sales, and used other questionable accounting practices to inflate earnings.[37] This particular manipulation was apparently widespread; an investigation concluded that a "substantial number" of the division's approximately 2,500 employees, including the division's top managers, either participated in the manipulation or were aware of it.

Still another example took place at Texaco. In 1979 the company had to reduce its stated oil reserves by 25 percent and its gas reserves by 16 percent because managers in the field were submitting optimistic estimates to appear as though they were doing well, and the estimates were not well scrutinized.[38]

What makes data manipulation feasible is a failure to make the measurements suitably objective. The adoption of "liberal" accounting methods is only feasible if management is allowed to choose its own indicators of performance — an obvious failure to satisfy the objectivity criterion. In the McCormick & Company situation, the investigators laid much too much of the blame for the inadequate objectivity on the failure of the outside auditors to perform their functions well. Their analytical review was deficient in that they did not pursue some of the observed improprieties far enough and they apparently did not sufficiently understand the division's accounting methods. But in many of the other situations, management is allowed to choose from among several acceptable measurement methods; so the manipulations of results measures are totally within the rules.

Manipulation is a very serious problem that seems to be growing worse. Manipulation is serious because it can render an entire control system ineffective; it no longer becomes possible to determine if a particular individual has done a good job. Its effects can also go far beyond the control system because it can destroy the accuracy of a company's entire information system. Manipulation seems to be a growing problem, perhaps because the difficult economic conditions most companies have faced in the last few years have made targets more difficult to attain and have thus added pressure for performance.[39]

OPERATING DELAYS

Operating delays are an often unavoidable consequence of the preaction review types of action controls and some of the forms of behavioral constraints. Delays such as those caused by limiting access to a stockroom or by requiring a signature check by an accounting clerk are usually minor, but other control-caused delays can be very major.

For example, after executives of the Harley-Davidson Motor Company bought the firm from AMF Inc., the director of marketing services boasted that a rebate program was instituted in ten days, rather than the six to eight weeks it would have taken with all the reviews necessary in the multileveled AMF hierarchy.[40] At Genesco, Inc., the retail and apparel conglomerate, approvals that were required were said to have "straitjacketed" operations, as delays "of only a few weeks resulted in the loss of precious selling time at the height of the season."[41] At Xerox Corporation, one manager complained that the checks and balances necessary to move from the conceptual to the detailed engineering phase of developing a new product took two years, instead of the two weeks to a month that should have been required.[42]

Obviously, where fast action is important, delays such as these can be significant. Delays are a major reason for the negative connotation associated with the word *bureaucracy*. In the organizations that tend to place more emphasis on the action controls and, as a consequence, suffer these bureaucratic operating delays, many control system changes are motivated by a desire to reduce the burdens caused by these types of controls. For example, when Helmut Maucher took over as the chief executive at Nestle (which ranks as number forty-three on *Fortune*'s list of industrial companies in the world), he diagnosed the company's major problems as "bigness — slow reaction time, a tendency to bureaucratic perfectionism, and a diffuseness of purpose." Maucher was quoted as saying that "the administrative system was somewhat 'heavy.' "[43]

A similar occurrence took place at the Honeywell Information Systems subsidiary of Honeywell, Inc. When James Renier was installed as the new president, his first action was to emphasize results controls at managerial levels in the organization. He set up new product divisions with profit-and-loss responsibility in order to allow managers "to develop and market new systems without the bureaucratic interference that has often slowed Honeywell in the past." The prior control system had "killed the entrepreneurial spirit . . . and many executives fled the slow-moving bureaucracy."[44]

Operating delays caused by controls are not an independent problem, of course; they can cause other managerial reactions that are probably not desirable. A recent survey of general managers in a well-run diversified corporation found that 74 percent obtained required approvals after the money was spent in order to speed up the process.[45]

NEGATIVE ATTITUDES

Controls can cause any of a number of negative attitudinal effects, including job tension, conflict, frustration, and resistance, even if the controls are well designed.[46] Such attitudes are important not only because they are indicators of employee welfare but also because they are coincident with many behaviors that can be harmful.[47]

The causes of negative attitudes are complex; they may be precipitated by any of a large number of factors such as economic conditions, organization structure, and administrative processes, alone and in combinations. Furthermore, these factors seem to affect different types of managers differently.

Action Controls and Negative Attitudes

Most people, particularly professionals, react negatively to the use of action controls. David Louks, controller at Lear Siegler, observed that over the years he and his staff had much greater opportunities to participate in preaction reviews of operations. He acknowledged that "this chafes line managers," but he went on to observe that "they're learning that controls are here to stay."[48]

Preaction reviews can be particularly frustrating if the managers being reviewed do not perceive the reviews as serving a useful purpose. This was apparently the situation at Fairchild Camera and Instrument after the company was bought by Schlumberger Ltd. A manager who left the company observed: "It got to be frustrating to get new ideas endorsed by, basically, an oil-field company that didn't have the foggiest notion of what high technology is really all about."[49]

Action controls can also annoy lower-level personnel. A junior employee at Atari, Inc., observed that

> Atari is run by telling people what to do and giving them almost no responsibility. That's why most of us just think of this as a great training ground and don't plan to stay.[50]

Results Controls and Negative Attitudes

Results controls can also produce negative attitudes. One factor that seems to produce them is the fact that the persons whose behaviors are being controlled often lack commitment to the goals defined in the control system. Most individuals are not committed to goals they consider too difficult, not meaningful, not controllable, unwise, illegal, or unethical.[51] For instance, in the example of a tight results control system presented in Chapter 6 — the system used at UPS — commitment seems low because the targets set are perhaps too difficult. While UPS has been very successful to date, there are some clouds on the horizon as some of the drivers compare their working conditions with those in a "Roman galley." The company has had some labor problems already, and although they have avoided major problems apparently because of very generous salaries, the drivers could rebel at some point; in fact, one driver recently forecast that "in 10 years this company is going to be in real trouble."[52]

Here is another such example. A manager who is concerned that the standards by which he is being judged are not fair remarked:

> We start the planning process at the beginning of the year. It takes 4–5 months. The 1982 plan was done in mid-1981, and that was quite a good year for us. I was forced to present an optimistic plan, because I couldn't go in with numbers that were lower than what we were doing. You always have to forecast some growth. But the recession hit us very hard in 1982, and I missed my plan by quite a large margin. That seems to reflect badly on my performance, but I don't think that's fair. I think the standard was wrong.[53]

Negative attitudes may also stem from problems in the measurement system. A lack of measurement precision tends to produce negative attitudes because it may perpetuate unfair performance evaluations, and it is common to hear managers complain that they are being held responsible for things over which they have little or no control.

> It is terribly frustrating to be evaluated as a profit center when I do not have complete control over revenues. The Export Division is responsible for over 75% of our total sales. They determine the price, the destination and the quantity of most of the milk we sell. We have no direct authority over that department, yet we are held responsible when sales are poor. If they do not perform up to expectations, then we cannot meet the budgeted profit target for which we are held responsible by headquarters.[54]

Other potential causes of negative attitudes may be associated with the rewards (or punishments) associated with the control system. For example, rewards that are not perceived to be equitable — and perhaps most forms of punishment — tend to produce any of a number of negative attitudes.[55]

Even the goal-setting and evaluation processes themselves may produce negative attitudes. Many authors suggest that results controls that are applied in conjunction with a people-insensitive, nonsupportive, or negative *leadership style* may tend to lower goal commitment and cause any of a number of negative attitudinal reactions.[56] Allowing employees to participate in setting their goals often reduces negative feelings toward results-oriented control systems.

Finally, just the process of changing results controls is annoying to many people. Companies that have acquired other companies have encountered this resistance. Xerox Corporation saw some of the managers of its two key high-technology acquisitions — Diablo Systems and Shugart Associates — resign in part because of frustration caused by the institution of new reporting procedures.[57]

The collection of factors affecting attitudes is very complex. There is some evidence that poor performers may react more negatively the better a control system is because the limitations in their abilities are easier to discover.[58] But more important are system flaws that could cause negative attitudes in potentially good performers. Attitudes are important outcomes of control systems to monitor not only because they have their own value as indicators of employee welfare but also because the presence of these negative attitudes may indicate the propensity to engage in any of a number of dysfunctional behaviors, such as feeding the systems invalid data or other forms of gamesmanship, withdrawal, or even sabotage. Each of the characteristics mentioned here as a possible cause of negative attitudes has been the focus of much research and the subject of more than one whole book. However, one important point that is clearly true is that the design of the structure of a control system does not guarantee its success; the implementation of the system is also an important determinant. The relationships between the styles of implementation and the attitudinal outcomes are highly contextual, and our knowledge of these effects is fragmentary.

CONCLUSION

Control system designers must be cognizant of the possibility of creating any of a wide variety of harmful side effects as they strive to create a good control environment. And these side effects can be significant; only 26 percent of the general managers who responded to the recent survey about controls disagreed with the following statement: "Overall, the controls have done more harm than good to the long-term success of my profit center."[59]

Four general observations can be made about the occurrence of these side effects. First, as the summary shown in Table 7.1 points out, the harmful side effects are not unique to one form of control. The risk of side effects does seem to be smaller where the personnel controls are used, however.

Second, some of the control types have negative side effects that are largely unavoidable. It is, for example, difficult, or even impossible, for people to enjoy following a strict set of procedures (action accountability) for a long period of time, although the negative attitudes can probably be minimized if the reasons for them are well communicated and if the list is kept to a minimum.

Third, the likelihood of severe dysfunctional side effects is greatest where there is either a failure to satisfy one or more of the desirable design criteria or a misfit between the type of control and the situation.

Fourth, where the possibility of dysfunctional effects exists, the tighter the degree of control applied, the greater the likelihood for dysfunctional side effects and the more severe the effects that will be felt:

> One fundamental reason control systems often fail and sometimes boomerang is that those who design them fail to understand that an important aspect of human behavior in an organizational setting is that noncompliance tends to appear in the presence of a perceived threat.[60]

This same observation has been made by a number of authors.[61]

What makes dealing with these potential problems so difficult is that there is not always a simple one-to-one relationship between the control type and the effect; furthermore, the existence of the side effects is often difficult to detect. For example, a failure to make the measurement processes objective in

Table 7.1. Control Types and Harmful Side Effects Possible

Type of Control	Behavioral Displacement	Gamesmanship	Operating Delays	Negative Attitudes
Results controls:				
Results accountability	X	X		X
Action controls:				
Behavioral constraint			X	X
Preaction review			X	X
Action accountability	X	X		X
Redundancy				X
Personnel controls:				
Selection and placement				
Training				
Culture	X			
Group-based rewards	X			
Provision of necessary resources				

a results or action accountability control system just presents the possibility for data manipulation; actual manipulation may not occur until an individual has a personal need for more money, poor performance creates additional pressure to perform, or a new, unfair leader creates a motivation to manipulate.

Another difficult factor to deal with is the fact that resistance to control systems is often based on misinformation.[62] Control system changes can generate great anxiety in the individuals to be affected, and if complete and accurate information is not provided and believed, some people may make inferences based on their incomplete information set and may behave in manners that appear irrational to an outside observer.

The combinations of factors that cause these side effects are admittedly complex. A more complete understanding will have to await the findings of more research.

NOTES

1. Steven Kerr, "On the Folly of Rewarding A While Hoping for B," *Academy of Management Journal* 18 (December 1975): 769–83.
2. Martin Landau and Russell Stout, Jr., "To Manage Is Not to Control: Or the Folly of Type II Errors," *Public Administration Review* 39 (March–April 1979): 148–56.
3. Chris Argyris, *The Impact of Budgets on People* (Ithaca, N.Y.: School of Business and Public Administration, Cornell University, 1952).
4. Peter M. Blau, *The Dynamics of Bureaucracy* (Chicago: University of Chicago Press, 1955).
5. John P. Kotter, Leonard A. Schlesinger, and Vijay Sathe, *Organization: Text, Cases, and Readings on the Management of Organizational Design and Change* (Homewood, Ill.: Richard D. Irwin, 1979), p. 25.
6. Eric Flamholtz, "Organizational Control Systems as a Managerial Tool," *California Management Review* XXII (Winter 1979): 50–59.
7. Regina Herzlinger, "The Hyatt Hill Health Center," case no. 9–172–309 (Boston: HBS Case Services, 1972).
8. Edward E. Lawler III and John G. Rhode, *Information and Control in Organizations* (Pacific Palisades, Calif.: Goodyear, 1976), p. 95.
9. N. Babchuk and W. J. Goode, "Work Incentives in a Self-Determined Group," *American Social Review* 16 (1951): 679–87.
10. V. F. Ridgway, "Dysfunctional Consequences of Performance Measurements," in *Information for Decision Making,* ed. Alfred Rappaport (Englewood Cliffs, N.J.: Prentice-Hall, 1982), pp. 378–83.
11. Charles H. Ford, "MBO: An Idea Whose Time Has Gone," *Business Horizons* 23 (December 1979): 54.
12. David Mitchell, *Control without Bureaucracy* (London: McGraw-Hill, 1979), p. 6.
13. Peter F. Drucker, "Controls, Control and Management," in *Management Controls:*

New Directions in Basic Research, ed. Charles P. Bonini, Robert K. Jaedicke, and Harvey M. Wagner (New York: McGraw-Hill, 1964), p. 294.

14. Stephen J. Sansweet, "Troubles at Mattel Seen Extending Beyond Fallout in Electronics Line," *Wall Street Journal,* December 1, 1983, p. 31.

15. Drucker, "Controls," p. 295.

16. Blau, *Dynamics of Bureaucracy.*

17. Adam Smith, *An Inquiry into the Nature and Causes of the Wealth of Nations* (1776; reprinted ed., Modern Library [Random House], 1937), p. 734.

18. Daniel Katz and Robert L. Kahn, *The Social Psychology of Organizations,* 2d ed. (New York: Wiley, 1978).

19. Michael B. McCaskey, *The Executive Challenge: Managing Change and Ambiguity* (Marshfield, Mass.: Pitman Publishing Inc., 1982), p. 112.

20. "A Takeover Hasn't Cramped Oppenheimer's Freewheeling Style," *Business Week,* October 10, 1983, p. 94.

21. Thomas J. Peters, "Putting Excellence into Management," *Business Week,* July 21, 1980, p. 205.

22. "Conglomerate Managers Fall into Step, Too," *Business Week,* February 6, 1984, p. 50.

23. Ibid., p. 54.

24. Betsy Morris, "After a Long Simmer, The Pot Boils Again at Campbell Soup Co.," *Wall Street Journal,* July 16, 1982, p. 1.

25. H. H. Meyer, "The Pay-for-Performance Dilemma," *Organizational Dynamics* 4 (Winter 1975): 39–50.

26. Robert S. Kaplan, dean of the Graduate School of Industrial Administration at Carnegie Mellon University, quoted in "Executive Compensation: Looking to the Long Term Again," *Business Week,* May 9, 1983, p. 81.

27. For example, see Richard M. Cyert and James G. March, *A Behavioral Theory of the Firm* (Englewood Cliffs, N.J.: Prentice-Hall, 1963).

28. Michael Schiff and Arie Y. Lewin, "Where Traditional Budgeting Fails," *Financial Executive* 36 (May 1968): 50–62.

29. Mohamed Onsi, "Factor Analysis of Behavioral Variables Affecting Budgetary Slack," *Accounting Review* XLVIII (October 1973): 535–48.

30. Geert H. Hofstede, *The Game of Budget Control* (Assen, The Netherlands: Van Gorcum, 1967).

31. Jay Galbraith, *Organization Design* (Reading, Mass.: Addison-Wesley, 1977).

32. Harold Wilensky, *Organizational Intelligence* (New York: Basic Books, 1967).

33. Eric Flamholtz, "Behavioral Aspects of Accounting/Control Systems," in *Organizational Behavior,* ed. Steven Kerr (Columbus, Ohio: Grid, 1979), pp. 289–316.

34. Kenneth A. Merchant, "The Effects of Organizational Controls" (Working Paper, Graduate School of Business Administration, Harvard University 1984).

35. George Getschow, "Slick Accounting Ploys Help Many Companies Improve Their Income," *Wall Street Journal,* June 20, 1980, p. 34.

36. Brenton R. Schlender, "Datapoint Kept Trying to Set Profit Records Until the Bubble Burst," *Wall Street Journal,* May 27, 1982, p. 1.

37. Betsy Morris, "McCormick & Co. Division Is Found to Use Dubious Accounting Methods to Boost Net," *Wall Street Journal,* June 1, 1982, p. 10.

38. "Texaco's Single-Minded Boss," *Business Week,* May 9, 1983, pp. 61–67.
39. Betsy Morris, "Accounting Scams Are on the Rise, Putting More Pressure on Auditors," *Wall Street Journal,* July 9, 1982, p. 19.
40. Heywood Klein, "At Harley-Davidson, Life without AMF Is Upbeat But Full of Financial Problems," *Wall Street Journal,* April 13, 1982, p. 37.
41. "The Controller: Inflation Gives Him More Clout with Management," *Business Week,* August 15, 1977, p. 95.
42. "The Shrinking of Middle Management," *Business Week,* April 25, 1983, p. 55.
43. Robert Ball, "A 'Shopkeeper' Shakes Up Nestlé," *Fortune,* December 27, 1982, p. 105.
44. "Honeywell's Survival Plan in Computers," *Business Week,* May 23, 1983, p. 111.
45. Merchant, "Effects."
46. Many authors have discussed this point. For example, see Argyris, *Impact of Budgets;* Blau, *Dynamics of Bureaucracy;* Cortlandt Cammann, "Effects of the Use of Control Systems," *Accounting, Organizations and Society* 16 (1976): 301–14; and Anthony G. Hopwood, *Accounting and Human Behaviour* (Englewood Cliffs, N.J.: Prentice-Hall, 1976).
47. This is a consistent area of agreement among the various attitude-behavior consistency theories, such as balance theory (for example, Fritz Heider, "Attitudes and Cognitive Organization," *Journal of Psychology* 21 [January 1946]: 107–12) and cognitive dissonance theory (such as, Jack W. Brehm and Arthur R. Cohen, *Explorations in Cognitive Dissonance* [New York: John Wiley, 1958]).
48. "The Controller," p. 86.
49. "Chip Wars: The Japanese Threat," *Business Week,* May 23, 1983, p. 85.
50. "Atari's Struggle to Stay Ahead," *Business Week,* September 13, 1982, p. 56.
51. For example, see Edwin A. Locke, Karyll N. Shaw, Lise M. Saari, and Gary Latham, "Goal Setting and Task Performance: 1969–1980," *Psychological Bulletin* 90 (1981): 125–52.
52. "Behind the UPS Mystique:" Puritanism and Productivity *Business Week,* June 6, 1983, p. 68.
53. Personal interview with a general manager in a large, diversified firm.
54. William A. Sahlman and M. Edgar Barrett, "Laitier, S.A.," case no. 9–176–118 (Boston: HBS Case Services, 1975).
55. For example, see Robert T. Keller and Andrew D. Szilagyi, "Employee Reactions to Leader Reward Behavior," *Academy of Management Journal* 19 (December 1976): 619–27; and Edward E. Lawler III, *Pay and Organization Development* (Reading, Mass.: Addison-Wesley, 1980).
56. See, for example, J. B. Ritchie and Raymond E. Miles, "An Analysis of Quantity and Quality of Participation as Mediating Variables in the Participative Decision-Making Process," *Personnel Psychology* 23 (1970): 347–59; Hopwood, *Accounting and Human Behavior;* David T. Otley, "Budget Use and Managerial Performance," *Journal of Accounting Research* 16 (Spring 1978): 122–49; Peter Brownell, "Participation in the Budgeting Process — When It Works and When It Doesn't," *Journal of Accounting Literature* 1 (Spring 1982): 124–53.
57. "The New Entrepreneurs," *Business Week,* April 18, 1983, p. 78.
58. Lawler and Rhode, *Information and Control.*

59. Merchant, "Effects."

60. Douglas McGregor, *The Professional Manager* (New York: McGraw-Hill, 1967), p. 8.

61. For example, see Cammann, "Effects" Hopwood, *Accounting and Human Behaviour*; Frank Collins, "The Interaction of Budget Characteristics and Personality Variables with Budgetary Response Attitudes," *Accounting Review* LIII (April 1978): 324–35; Jacob Y. Kamin and Joshua Ronen, "Effects of Budgetary Control Design on Management Decisions: Some Empirical Evidence," *Decision Sciences* 12 (July 1981): 471–85.

62. Lawler and Rhode, *Information and Control*.

chapter eight

FINANCIAL ACCOUNTABILITY CONTROL: ISSUES AND APPROACHES

This chapter focuses in detail on the advantages and disadvantages of financial accountability control (FAC). FAC is a form of results control that involves holding managers accountable for results defined in monetary (usually accounting) terms, such as net income, earnings per share, and/or return on investment, assets, or equity.

This special focus on FAC is warranted because it is probably the single most important type of control used in large business firms, and it is particularly important for controlling the actions of managers. FAC is used extensively even at lower levels of management because as corporations grow, they tend to adopt decentralized forms of organization with relatively independent financial responsibility centers (for example, profit or investment centers).[1] The vast majority of the short-term (one-year) and long-term (multiple-year) compensation plans used in these entities pay for achievement of targets for net income or growth in earnings per share.[2] Since the recession in the early 1980s, the trend in the United States, at least, seems to be toward providing a higher proportion of compensation based on performance-based incentives.[3]

However, while FAC has some undeniable advantages, it also has some disadvantages that have caused it to come under considerable criticism recently for, among other things, causing managers to overemphasize short-term performance. After outlining the advantages, this chapter describes the potential problems that can be caused by the use of FAC and some of the approaches companies have taken to capitalize on the advantages of FAC while minimizing the disadvantages.

THE ADVANTAGES OF FINANCIAL
ACCOUNTABILITY CONTROLS

There are several very good reasons for the ubiquity of FAC in business organizations. First, it is natural for business firms to monitor success in financial terms because financial objectives are among these organizations' most important objectives. Financial measures of success are potentially useful not only for directing and evaluating managerial actions but also for analyzing the success of the strategies that have been chosen.

Second, FAC can provide a relatively easy and inexpensive way for upper-level managers to ensure that everything is working as they had hoped. Often only one (or just a few) results measures can provide a good summary of the effects of most of the actions that managers need to control. It then becomes unnecessary to track each action that can affect financial performance (for example, how time was spent, how specific expenditures were made), or to track the specific line items that affect the summary measures of performance, until problems (such as, negative variances) appear in the summary measures. As a consequence the amount of information that managers need to assimilate is reduced. This is the basis for what is generally known as *management by exception*.

Third, utilizing FAC is a method of control that can be effective even when management does not know what specific actions are best, as is often the case in uncertain environments and with jobs that require considerable professional judgment.

Fourth, FAC can provide a relatively subtle or unobtrusive form of control. It provides control while allowing those being controlled considerable autonomy. This freedom of action allows managers to adapt their operations to fit their managerial styles, and it may stimulate creative thinking.

Fifth, the cost of implementing FAC is often small relative to that of other forms of control. This is because the core elements of FAC — the measures of financial performance — are largely in place if the organization can use or adapt measures that are required to be sent to government agencies, creditors, shareholders, and/or potential investors.

POTENTIAL PROBLEMS WITH FINANCIAL ACCOUNTABILITY CONTROLS

In some situations, however, use of FAC causes negative side effects so damaging that they outweigh the advantages. The most serious problems are several forms of behavioral displacement and gamesmanship. The following sections discuss these problems, what causes them, and what some companies have done to try to avoid or alleviate them.

Behavioral Displacement

As discussed in the last chapter, behavioral displacement occurs where the control system induces behaviors that are not consistent with what the organization wants. Two forms of displacement are particularly worrisome where FAC is used: management myopia and excessive risk aversion.

Management Myopia

One criticism of FAC that has been made frequently in the last few years is that American firms, in particular, are using control systems that cause managers to be overly focused on short-term profits at the expense of their longer-term strategic obligations. This problem can be termed the *management myopia problem*. The following are typical of the criticisms that have been made:

> [American managers] have let their time horizons — the time over which projects must pay for themselves — become so short that they will not undertake the basic research and development, make the necessary investments, or build the service networks necessary for long-term survival."[4]

> By their preference for servicing existing markets rather than creating new ones and by their devotion to short-term returns and "management by the numbers," many [American managers] have effectively foresworn long-term technological superiority a competitive weapon. In consequence, they have abdicated their strategic responsibilities."[5]

> [American managers] "do not have a long term commitment to growth that permits delayed gratification."[6]

Much of the blame for this management myopia has been attributed — by a broad set of critics in business, academia, and government — to the FACs that are used extensively in all but the smallest business organizations. For example, a panel of 230 chief executives assembled by *Dun's Business Month* blamed much of the reduction in the competitive strength of U.S. business on "outside pressure for quarter-to-quarter performance."[7] An award-winning *Harvard Business Review* article noted that "maximum short-term financial returns have become the overriding criteria for many companies."[8] Lyman Hamilton, former chief executive of ITT who now heads the privately owned Tamco Enterprises, observed:

> Every C.E.O. says he plans for long term. But every C.E.O. lies. He's always temporizing with quarterly earnings. If he doesn't hack it quarter to quarter, he doesn't survive.[9]

William Norris, chairman and chief executive officer of Control Data Corporation, wrote:

> [Most large corporations have avoided] long-term, large-scale, high-risk investments in new products, services, and processes [because of] investor pressure for immediate earnings and executive bonuses keyed primarily to annual performance."[10]

And Nolan Bushnell, chairman of Pizza Time Theater Inc. and founder of Atari Inc., noted:

> Because of shareholder pressures for short-term profits, American managers' jobs are too precariously balanced on this quarter's results to take the risks needed to fuel successful product development. American companies have beaten themselves.[11]

As it is widely believed that FAC is one of the primary causes of management myopia, it is useful to ask what it is about FAC that cause management myopia. Only when the causes are understood can the important, practical question as to whether myopia is an inevitable side effect of the use of FAC or whether it is brought about by an inappropriate use of FAC be answered.

It appears that myopia, which is a form of displacement, is caused by the same factors discussed in Chapter 7 as the primary causes of displacement. In particular, the measures of performance in common use in FAC systems can be described as being incongruent, in that myopic behaviors are rewarded, and/ or incomplete, in that long-term-oriented behaviors are not rewarded.

It is generally agreed that the true financial objective of business organizations is *to increase owners' wealth*.[12] Ownership wealth (company value) can be calculated in the same way any asset is valued; that is, by discounting the expected future cash flows for the time value of money and risk. Therefore, managers should serve the owners of the firm by taking steps to increase the future cash flow potentials and to decrease the risk. The change in value (shareholder wealth) over any given period is called *economic income,* and an alternative way of phrasing the basic corporate financial objective is maximization of economic income — not *accounting income,* meaning revenues less expenses, both as defined by accountants.

The understanding of this financial objective is very important because it defines how congruence is to be judged; we can say that the congruence of any measure of financial performance of a business organization should be judged by the extent to which it provides an accurate assessment of economic income. This is now generally accepted, even by accounting rule-making bodies, such as the Financial Accounting Standards Board:

> The ideal measure of the worth of the resources of an enterprise might be obtained by measuring assets at the net present value of future cash flows. An asset is valuable to the extent that it can generate future cash flows and only to that extent. Moreover, if net present values would be ideal measures of worth, changes in net present values over a period would be ideal measures of enterprise performance.[13]

The important FAC evaluation question, then, is, How well do the surrogate measures used most commonly in financial accountability control systems, which are usually phrased in accounting terms (for example, growth in net income, return on assets, or return on equity), meet the congruence criterion? The answer is: Not very well!!!

The congruence weaknesses of accounting measures of performance have been discussed and demonstrated both on theoretical and empirical grounds by both practitioners and academics.[14] The problems result because accounting measures of performance have many limitations, including these:

- They are primarily a summation of the effects of the transactions that took place during a given period. Most changes in value that do not result in a transaction are not recognized in income.
- They are highly dependent on the choice of measurement method, and multiple measurement methods are often available to account for identical economic events.
- They ignore the time value of money.
- They ignore risk and changes in risk.
- They are dependent on measurement rules that are sometimes heavily biased toward conservatism.

- They ignore the economic worth of companies' intangible assets, such as the research in progress, people, and the goodwill that has been built up.
- They focus on the past, with no guarantee that past performance is a reliable indicator of future performance.

These kinds of theoretical limitations should be expected to cause accounting measures of performance to be poor indicators of economic performance, and the best evidence that is available suggests that this is indeed the case. The best objective indicators of economic values are the market values in actively traded stock markets with many informed traders, such as the large U.S. stock markets, and accounting earnings changes have been shown not to provide reliable indicators of market value changes. A recent review of the studies focused on this issue found that the average correlation between annual percentage changes in accounting earnings and annual percentage changes in market prices was only approximately 0.38.[15] While it is encouraging that the sign of this correlation is positive, its small size means that changes in annual accounting earnings "explain" only a small proportion (<20 percent) of the variance of returns provided to shareholders or, perhaps, explain them only after some time lag.

The practical significance of this low correlation was shown in a recent study of the 172 firms of Standard & Poor's 400 industrial companies that had earnings per share growth (excluding extraordinary items) of 15 percent or greater over the period from 1974 to 1979. In 27 (16 percent) of these firms, shareholders realized negative nominal rates of return (dividends less capital losses) over this period, despite the healthy earnings pattern. And shareholders in 60 of the 172 firms (35 percent) had negative real returns (that is, returns inadequate to compensate them for inflation).[16]

The degree of congruence is not constant across firms. In general, it is worse for firms with long production cycles and a relatively small number of large sales transactions, but it can vary significantly with some of the accounting policies chosen (for example, capitalization and depreciation policies, inventory accounting method).[17]

It is true that accounting measures of performance have been used as the basis for FACs for many years, and yet the criticisms are relatively recent; so a logical question is, What is different now? The answer seems obvious: The correlations between accounting income and economic income are probably much lower now than in earlier decades.

This deterioration in the congruence of accounting income measures of performance is probably true for two basic reasons. First, economic values have been changing much more rapidly in recent years owing to, for example, relatively high environmental volatility, inflation rates that have been high by historical standards and that have fluctuated erratically, and foreign currency exchange rates that have been allowed to float only since 1973. Accounting measurement rules tend to smooth income — for example, by spreading the cost of fixed assets over a large number of periods — and the accounting measures of performance will not recognize the volatility in economic values in a timely manner.

Second, over the years the accounting rules have been made more uniform, ostensibly to improve precision and comparability across firms. But, uniformity has its costs; it can make different economic realities appear the same. A good example is Financial Accounting Standard no. 2, which requires that expenditures on research and development be expensed immediately.[18] This rule has improved precision but has been criticized by many for obscuring the economic reality.[19]

The effects of these accounting measurement weaknesses can be severe, as they cause managers to be misled by their own information. In the 1800s railroads used a form of cash-based accounting (called *replacement accounting*) that did not require expensing the costs of assets (such as, through depreciation) until assets were replaced. The effect was that "stockholders were misled as to actual income, future earnings potential, and managerial efficiency."[20] But perhaps more important, the railroad managers themselves seemed to be fooled by the numbers, as they were motivated to defer the replacement of worn-out equipment to boost earnings, and this probably contributed to the fact that half of the track mileage constructed in the United States before 1900 was ultimately placed in receivership.[21] This constitutes a severe example of managers emphasizing the short run at the expense of the long run.

The conclusion, then, must be that the potential indeed exists for FAC to cause management myopia. Several ways in which this problem might be alleviated are discussed at the end of this chapter.

Excessive Risk Aversion

The congruence failures of FAC also tend to cause a problem known generally as *excessive risk aversion*. This problem has been widely discussed in the managerial accounting, finance, and economics literatures,[22] and it is receiving increasing recognition in the popular management literature.[23]

Excessive risk aversion arises because shareholders are, for the most part, risk neutral, whereas most managers, who are hired to act in the shareholders' best interests, seem to be risk averse. Shareholders do not need individual firms to pursue diversification because they can easily and inexpensively diversify their risk in the capital markets. Managers, however, are induced to be risk averse because their rewards are tied to the success of only one firm (ignoring the possibilities they might have in an open labor market). Therefore, they are motivated to pass up some worthwhile but risky opportunities and to add complementary lines of business.[24] Diversification creates shareholder value only if it creates operating synergies or economies of scale. If diversification is costly and pursued to reduce the entity's exposure to partially random outcomes, it is bad.

The cause of excessive risk aversion, like that of management myopia, is also the congruence failures of the measures of performance commonly within FAC. Instead of rewarding managers for taking prudent risks, the controls used in most companies actually discourage risk taking. Managers are often punished for negative variances from plan but are not necessarily rewarded for positive variances. Furthermore, they often have to justify every significant expenditure. These controls discourage risk taking.

Gamesmanship

As in Chapter 7, the term *gamesmanship* is used to refer generally to the actions that managers take that are intended to improve their measures of performance without effecting any positive economic effects. These games need not be myopic, as the short run is not necessarily being emphasized at the expense of the long run, and they may or may not include direct manipulation of measures.

Most of the managerial games are only possible because of failures of the accounting measures of performance to meet one or more of the criteria of good performance measures, particularly congruence, precision, and/or objectivity. Actually, the measurement failures of FAC not only make gamesmanship possible but they often encourage managers to play the games so that the measures of their performances will be more "fair" and, hence, so too will be the evaluations made of them.

Congruence Failures and Gamesmanship

The following examples of managerial games all derive from congruence failures of the measures used in FAC systems:

- A manager depleted his stocks of spare parts and heating oil at year's end to reduce expenses even though he knew they would have to be bought back shortly thereafter (in the new fiscal year) at higher prices.[25]
- A company overshipped products to its distributors at year's end so that man-

agement could meet its budget targets even though it was known that the products would be returned.[26]

- Two division managers in a large firm sold parcels of land back and forth to each other so that the increases in economic value could be recognized as accounting income.[27]

- A manager bought equipment from an outside supplier, rather than from an in-company department, which could have done the job just as well, so that the design portion of the project could be capitalized.[28]

These games are all rooted in, and even encouraged by, congruence failures of accounting measures of performance. The first and second examples are of performance-smoothing actions that increase accounting earnings in the current period but actually decrease the economic value of the entity and the firm. The behavior in the third example is brought about because accounting measures of performance do not, in general, capture changes in economic values that do not result in a transaction; as a consequence, managers can "save" increases in values (real and nominal) and use them when accounting income is needed by completing a transaction. The behavior in the fourth example is brought about because the distinction accountants make between investments that must be capitalized and those that must be expensed is not based on economic grounds.

Unfortunately, games such as these are common even in well-run firms. Of the general managers of the well-run firm who responded to a recent study of controls, most admitted they had "pulled profits from future periods into the current period" — 91 percent by deferring a needed expenditure and 83 percent by accelerating a sale.[29]

Precision and Objectivity Failures and Gamesmanship

Precision and objectivity failures of results measures also rank as common causes of managerial gamesmanship. These problems are discussed together because while they are conceptually distinct, the two problems often occur together in practice, except where detailed audits are used to provide an objectivity check.

Despite the way they appear to nonaccountants, many accounting measures of performance are neither precise nor objective. In recent years this point has received considerable attention in the management literature.[30] The primary sources of imprecision in accounting measures are the "accounting judgments" that have to be made as to how economic events should be treated. Some economic events require no accounting judgments,[31] but for many other events, several allowable accounting alternatives exist, and the judgments leave room for manipulation.

For example, accounting for capital equipment expenditures requires judgments as to what qualifies as being capital (such as, minimum dollar amount, whether or not an "asset" has been created), the period of time over which the costs will be spread, and the method of depreciation (for example, straight-line, double-declining balance). Different judgments can have very significant effects on the bottom line (net income). In the long run, these differences will even out (assuming away the problem of the changing size of the unit of measure), but the pattern of earnings shown during the interim can be very misleading.

Most firms are able to avoid the most severe problems that these accounting judgments might cause by legislating "artificial precision." That is, they at least make the judgments consistently by defining exactly how certain events are to be measured and reducing the number of people who are allowed to make accounting measurement choices. In doing this, they reduce one significant element of randomness in the measures.

There is a limit as to how far the legislation of precision can be taken, of course. Different economic events require different treatments, and by limiting the number of accounting choices available, it is possible to increase precision at the same time the usefulness of the measurement is decreasing. Auditors are particularly anxious to emphasize precision at the expense of usefulness; "they sometimes prefer to try to apply one measurement method to everything."[32] At the extreme, accounting measures can be made perfectly precise, such as by generating a fixed set of numbers (such as, zero — expense everything), but the precision is gained at the expense of the utility of the information that might have been provided about significant economic events.

Since many difficult accounting judgments must be made, objectivity is very important. Can we say at least that accounting measures are objective? The answer to this question depends mostly on the measurement constraints applied to the managers whose performances are being measured, and these constraints vary in different parts of the firm. At top management levels, objectivity can be considered only fair, at best, because top-level managers have considerable discretion to select their own rules of measurement within the somewhat flexible limits of generally accepted accounting principles and the boundaries applied by the board of directors. Many books and articles have been written about managers' attempts to smooth, or otherwise influence, accounting measures of performance.[33] Examples of data manipulation are constantly being discovered, and there is evidence to suggest that the practice may be becoming more prevalent.[34]

At middle management levels, however, objectivity is somewhat better. Managers who are being evaluated on their achievement of financial results are generally not allowed much discretion to choose their own accounting methods, and the choices that they do make are reviewed by staff in the controller and internal audit organizations. Despite these constraints, however, some subjectivity is inevitable, as managers are sometimes in the best position to make the judgments that underlie the accounting measures.

For example, measuring performance of entities that work on a relatively small number of large projects (for example, job shops) provides some particularly difficult problems for accountants. Most job shops that work on large projects use percentage-completion accounting. But the persons in the best position to estimate the percentage complete and the estimated costs to completion are the project and entity managers; so accountants either have to trust the estimates they are given or bring in their own technical experts to review the work at what could be considerable expense.

In some situations completed-contract accounting is an acceptable measurement alternative. This alternative seems to provide increased precision because it is easy to verify the critical event — completion — and by the time of completion, most of the expenses will have been paid. But consider the following comments from the manager of a department of a large corporation that uses complete-contract accounting:

> This department is subject to extreme cyclical swings because we produce capital equipment primarily. In the last two recessions, our revenue dropped sharply, and we had to lay off 30–40% of our people, and these were good technical people who are hard to replace. I think it makes sense to keep as many of these people employed as we can, even if there are periods when they are not as busy as we might like.
>
> Fortunately, we have had some good years since the last recession and have been able to build up a cushion. We do this by being very conservative with our accounting. We don't take billings on a project until the last possible moment; that is, we keep it on the books until we are sure that all of the costs have been incurred. In addition, we are able to subtract projected losses from income as soon as they are forecast, so we are very conservative with our estimates of the costs that will be required to complete projects. You might say that our accounting for every project is on a "worst-possible-case" basis. This keeps our inventory values low and provides an ultra-conservative income statement.
>
> I think conservatism has a positive effect. If our revenues turn down again, as I'm sure they will, we will be able to meet the financial targets that we have to commit to for a while with the profits we have stored up. They might save some people's jobs.[35]

This example provides just one illustration of how easy it is to manipulate the accounting measures of performance, even within the constraints of the generally accepted accounting principles. The manager may be right — perhaps skilled people should be retained during slack periods — but it should not be necessary to manipulate the data so as to produce the correct result.

Unfortunately, this is not an isolated example. The revenue-recognition and allowances-for-future-losses issues faced in project accounting are difficult for accountants to deal with, but they are by no means the only problems. Manipulations are possible almost anywhere accounting judgments are necessary.

POSSIBLE SOLUTIONS

The problems that have been discussed in this chapter — management myopia, excessive risk aversion, and gamesmanship — can be solved, or at least alleviated. To this end, well-run companies seem to employ one or a combination of four types of solutions: improvements to accounting measures of performance, use of value-based performance measures, supplementation or replacement of FAC with nonfinancial measures of performance, and abandonment of results control.

Improvement of Accounting Measures

The accounting measures of performance can sometimes be redefined so that they better reflect cash flow potentials. This can be accomplished within the traditional historical cost-accounting framework, or it might involve a new framework such as inflation accounting or human resource accounting.

Within the Historical Cost-Accounting Framework

In some situations, measurement improvements can be effected through working within the existing historical cost-accounting framework, by choosing measurement rules that better reflect, or at least are not a direct contradiction to, the economic reality, or by lengthening the period over which performance is measured.

Choice of Better Measurement Rules. The accounting rules that are used for control purposes may be changed in any of a number of potentially beneficial ways. For example, setting up results reports for control purposes might require capitalization of expenditures for research and development, and for advertising and sales promotion, as the assumption could be made (until proven wrong) that those expenditures will result in cash flows in future periods (as they should if they are good investments). This accounting treatment is explicitly prohibited in the conservatively-biased rules required for external financial-reporting purposes despite the fact that it provides a "better matching of revenues and expenses" if in fact the future revenues are forthcoming. Similarly, internal reports for control purposes might also require the use of annuity (reverse-accelerated) depreciation, instead of the methods allowed for financial-reporting purposes (such as, straight-line, double-declining balance) because, many authors have maintained, this measurement method also provides a better approximation of the economic reality.[36]

While these changes can provide results measures that are better for control purposes than are the rules required by the financial-reporting rule-making bodies (for example, in the United States, the FASB and the Securities and Exchange Commission [SEC]), they can be costly to implement. Another set of financial records is required, and the added expense might not be inconsequential.

Another possibility is to challenge the rule-making bodies to try to get the rules changed. These challenges occur often, as accounting rule making in the United States is an overtly political process. An interesting, recent and highly publicized challenge was made by Comserv Corporation, a $23 million (revenues) computer software company. Comserv challenged the rule requiring the expensing of the costs of developing computer software, which, many accountants maintain, is just a form of research and development. Comserv maintained that its software development should be capitalized because the company was not speculating — it was dealing in a proven technology and the company knew that the products would be salable. Richard Daly, Comserv's chief executive officer (CEO) argued that "to expense it would be misleading; it would suggest we were shooting in the dark," and he went on to note that requiring the expensing of software costs can be damaging because it "inhibits a company from spending as much as it should."[37] While Comserv management has not been successful in getting the accounting rule changed, the SEC has temporarily allowed the company (and others that capitalized software development costs) to continue using its own measurement rules pending further discussions.[38]

Lengthening the Measurement Period. Another alternative that can be used to improve the congruence of the accounting measures of performance is to lengthen the period of measurement. Up to a point, it has been argued, the longer the period of measurement, the more congruent the accounting measures of performance.[39] Therefore, for example, annual accounting income should be, on average, a better indicator of annual economic income than quarterly accounting income is of quarterly economic income. This is because many of the accounting measurement rules tend to "smooth" the significant short-term fluctuations in economic income, and the effect is that the accounting measures are slow to respond to real economic changes.

In the last decade, quite a few companies have recognized this fact and attempted to extend their managers' horizons by implementing long-term incentive plans. These plans come in a variety of forms, but they usually provide rewards for the accomplishment of three- to six-year performance targets, expressed in terms such as earnings per share or accounting return on equity, sales, or assets. These plans have become quite popular in large firms; by 1981 performance-unit plans had been adopted by 82 of the 200 largest U.S. industrial companies.[40]

While these long-term plans have been in place only a short time, the evidence available suggests that implementation of the plans has the desirable effect of lengthening managerial horizons and, hence, combating management myopia. A recent study compared a sample of 25 firms that had adopted a performance plan between 1971 and 1978 with a matched sample of firms that had not adopted such a plan and found that a significant increase in capital investment followed the plan adoption and that security markets reacted favorably when the adoption of the plan was disclosed publicly.[41]

While extending the period of measurement does avoid some of the congruence problems of accounting measures of performance, several possible disadvantages exist. One is that the long-term incentives may drive much of the creative thinking out of strategic planning because most plans are calibrated by comparison with the long-term plans. This potential problem was a major concern of a financial vice-president at a large company that recently implemented a long-term incentive plan:

> I am worried that the new plan won't accomplish what we want, and it may even be counter-productive. We are a highly decentralized firm, and the instructions we send to our division presidents about how they are to do strategic planning emphasize the fact that we want it to be a creative process. We say: "We want you to 'blue-sky' and theorize. You tell us, as an entrepreneur, where you want to take the business. Assume the money is there." Now we are saying that the managers' long-term compensation is based on the strategic planning numbers. We may be eliminating any chance of getting the blue-sky thinking the company wants and really does need.[42]

Indeed, this manager's concern may be well placed. A sample of division managers in this company was interviewed, and they agreed that they were likely to present more conservative long-term plans.[43]

Other questions about long-term incentives also stand unanswered. For example, Do the rewards that are promised far into the future lose much of their motivational impact? How can companies induce their managers to transfer from a healthy division to one that needs to be turned around?

Inflation Accounting

Some firms use or are experimenting with replacement cost accounting (or the very similar current value accounting) in an effort to improve their measures of managerial performance. Replacement cost accounting is a form of inflation accounting that includes increases in asset values in income when the increases are recognized, not when they are realized as the result of the completion of a transaction, and provides for depreciation based on asset replacement values, not historical values. It has the advantage of segregating the gains that are due to holding assets in periods of inflation (that is, "holding" gains) that should not be consumed (such as, given out as compensation or dividends) if the company wishes to retain its real capital.

Some companies, including three giant European multinationals — Philips Industries N.V., Nestlé, and Ciba-Geigy — have used replacement cost accounting for many years, with good success. In the United States the list of companies that have experimented with replacement cost accounting measures of performance is short, but it does include General Electric,[44] American Standard,[45] FMC,[46] and TRW.[47]

It is too early to judge how successful these efforts might eventually be. Theoretically, replacement cost accounting provides better performance measurements than historical cost accounting, as John Grant, American Standard's executive vice-president, explained:

> [Replacement cost accounting performance reports will show management] whether a corporation under its stewardship is liquidating itself and, if not, to what extent it is generating funds for real growth.[48]

Most academics have supported the theory behind inflation accounting and have been surprised that it has not received a better reception from practitioners. One prominent academic recently restated the argument in favor of replacement cost accounting and suggested that one possible reason why more companies have not adopted it is management's ignorance of the defects of historical cost accounting.[49]

To date, however, there is no general agreement as to the desirability of inflation accounting. Early empirical research on the data required by FASB Statement no. 33[50] to be disclosed suggests that replacement cost accounting provides poorer indicators of shareholder returns (economic income) than does historical cost accounting, although this may be due to the experimental, and thus noncomparable, nature of the data used in the analyses.[51] And skepticism runs rampant among practitioners. Management of Winn-Dixie stores observed in the company's 1982 annual report that "the cost incurred to develop this [inflation-accounting] information far exceeds any benefit derived."

Human Resource Accounting

Human resource accounting (HRA) is another alternative that has been suggested as a possible improvement over historical cost-accounting measures of performance. HRA attempts to track changes in the values of the human assets in a firm, which are, proponents argue, many firms' most valuable assets. Considerable theoretical work has gone into ways of effecting HRA,[52] and a few firms, notably the R. G. Barry Corporation, have experimented with some aspects of its use, particularly the capitalization and subsequent amortization of training costs. However, as the precision of measurement of people-related factors is low, HRA has not been generally considered to be an alternative worthy of implementation.

Utilization of Value-Based Performance Measures

Another major category of measurement alternatives that can be used at the core of FAC systems can be called *value-based performance measures*. They are value based because instead of using backward-looking, transactions-oriented accounting reports they use estimates of changes in company values (cash flow potentials), using market prices or forecasts of future cash flows.

Market Value Measures

During the 1950s and 1960s stock price was the primary measure of company performance, and stock options were an important part of managerial incentive plans. Their importance declined significantly in the early 1970s because of poor stock market performance and a change in the tax laws. But since the late

1970s, options and other stock price–based compensation schemes — such as stock appreciation rights, phantom stock, and restricted stock — have again become popular.

The advantages of using stock price–based plans for control purposes is obvious. Congruence between managers' goals and those of the shareholders is immediately realized because the managers are rewarded in direct proportion to the actual market returns provided. Furthermore, the measures of performance are both precise and objective.

But several significant disadvantages exist. One is the controllability problem. Stock prices are affected by many factors that are not under even top management's control, including environmental conditions, competitors' actions, and acts of nature. Thus it is possible that the stock value changes may not provide a good reflection as to how effective the managers' actions are; outstanding managerial performance might not be reflected in higher stock returns, and poor managerial performance might be obscured by good stock performance. One way to avoid part of this problem is to adjust the individual companies' market movements by the amount of the general market movements, and perhaps also the industry effects; it is not possible to make accurate corrections for all uncontrollable influences, however.

Another problem is a serious feasibility limitation. Objective stock prices do not exist for firms that are not publicly held or that are traded only infrequently. And more important for most firms, stock returns are not useful for motivating individual middle managers, except perhaps as part of a companywide profit-sharing plan, because it is unlikely that any middle manager can have a perceptible effect on the stock price, even with truly outstanding (or very poor) performance.

Thus, we might conclude that stock price–based measures of performance are an alternative that should be considered only for top management in publicly held firms. Even in this situation, however, there is a question as to whether they provide useful performance indicators because of the controllability problem.

Discounted Cash Flow Estimates of Economic Income

Another possibility is to try to measure economic income itself by estimating changes in cash flow potentials and discounting them to a present value. Most people's first reaction to this possibility is negative, as it would seem to be very difficult to carry out in practice. But further consideration leads some to suggest that it might be workable within usable levels of accuracy in some situations.

Estimating future cash flows and discounting them to a present value is not a new problem in management. Most companies have considerable experience in preparing estimates of future cash flows and in reviewing the estimates for reasonableness. Potential cash flows are a standard part of investment and acquisition proposals, and some companies are also experimenting with using discounted cash flow methods for strategic planning of business units.[53]

Cash flow estimates, sometimes even including discounting of future inflows, are even an important part of many accounting rules despite the importance accountants place on measurement precision and verifiability. The most obvious example is reserve recognition accounting (RRA), which was required of firms in the oil industry for several years.[54] RRA was a type of economic income-based performance measure based on changes in estimates of future cash flows.[55] Discounted cash flow concepts are also part of the accounting rules for long-term receivables and liabilities since the face values of these items have to be discounted to present values at the time of the recording of the transaction. One of the significant trends in accounting actually seems to be a greater tolerance for this so-called soft, but more relevant, data.[56]

Recently, some authors have called for the use of discounted cash flow measures of performance because they are more congruent but not necessarily more vulnerable to manipulation.[57] Some managers seem to agree. A vice-president of a large manufacturing and distribution firm that was moving toward implementation of a discounted cash flow measurement system commented:

> We have become convinced that for [our company] at least, the traditional accounting measures, such as net earnings or return on net assets, are neither good criteria on which to base decisions, nor reliable indicators of performance. . . . We think that in evaluating possible actions, it is more important to focus on the possible impacts of future cash flows and risk, rather than estimating the impact on the accounting indicators. In addition, we think that it makes sense to judge our performance based on what we accomplish for our shareholders — meaning the amount of value we generate for them.[58]

Similarly, the president of a major division of an intermediate-sized oil company defended his company's use of incentives for explorationists (geologists and geophysicists) based on estimates of the net present value of new oil and gas reserves discovered but still in the ground by recalling an exchange he had had with critics of the bonus plan:

> Some of the people think it's nutty. They said: "Look at how you can manipulate those numbers." I replied: "Of course you can, but you can't manipulate [net present value] any more than you can manipulate many ac-

counting numbers. As long as you can trace the assumptions and origins of the numbers, anyone can figure out if you're lying, cheating or stealing, by and large."[59]

So, while some firms are beginning to consider some forms of economic income measures for control purposes,[60] measurement precision and objectivity are still significant stumbling blocks. But it is possible that direct estimates of economic income (that is, changes in cash flow potentials) may be a growing part of FAC systems in the future.

Deemphasis of Financial Accountability Control

Sometimes the best solution seems to be to deemphasize FAC. A number of academics have recently called for managers to look beyond the "bottom line." They have warned managers and investors that the pressures for constantly increasing quarterly earnings can be dysfunctional. Robert Kaplan, dean of the Graduate School of Industrial Administration at Carnegie-Mellon University, suggested that top managers should publicly give some version of the following message:

> The goal of this firm is not to exhibit steady predictable earnings growth. Rather our goal is to become a dominant force in our product markets. This strategy will require steady investments in research, product development, process improvements, and employee training that will be made even during downturns in the economy. A strategy of stable investments will increase the operating leverage of the firm, since more expenditures will be considered fixed rather than discretionary. Also, dividend increases may be limited, since operating cash flows will be redeployed within the firm. But in the long run, we are convinced that this strategy will create more value for the firm, its shareholders, its employees, and all the other constituents of the firm: customers, suppliers, and local communities. Therefore, the strategy must be evaluated on the firm's long-run profitability and dominant market position. For those investors for whom steady earnings are important, our firm is probably not a good one to hold in your investment portfolio. Only purchase and hold our shares if you are comfortable with our strategy of maximizing long-term capital gains. We will regularly provide you with operating statistics to keep you informed about our progress in becoming the most innovative or the most efficient producer in our product lines.[61]

Some managers, it seems, came up with the same idea on their own. Joe Henson, president and CEO of Prime Computer, Inc., noted at the 1983 shareholders meeting that "Prime is willing to sacrifice sequential quarterly earnings gains in order to invest in the long-term, future success of the company."[62] Steven Jobs, chairman of Apple Computer, stated that Apple is "absolutely prepared to sacrifice short-term profits to emerge from the shakeout [in small-computer manufacturers]."[63] And management of Signode Corporation, formerly so "preoccupied with meeting quarterly financial goals [that] it avoided high-risk investments whose payoff might be years down the road,"[64] has now chosen to make more long-term investments despite the negative short-term impact on net income.

Managers take many approaches when they decide to deemphasize FAC. Sometimes they use FAC for controlling operating performance only. At other times when FAC is deemphasized, they use other forms of results control such as nonfinancial indicators of performance or subjective assessments of performance. Still other times, they abandon results controls in favor of action and/or personnel controls. These alternatives are discussed in the following sections.

Use of FAC for Control of Operating Performance Only

Some companies (for example, Texas Instruments) find it useful to limit the use of FAC to control of day-to-day operating performance only. This requires segregating the measures of short-term, or operating, income from total income, as illustrated in Table 8.1. The key is to distinguish between operating expenses, which are necessary to produce the current period's revenue, and development expenses, which are incurred in order to generate revenues in future

Table 8.1. Isolation of Operating (short-term) Performance

Income Statement	Dollars
Standard:	
Revenue	100
Expenses	90
Net income	10
With operating performance isolated:	
Revenue	100
Operating expenses	50
Operating margin	50
Developmental expense	40
Net income	10

periods. If this distinction can be made, operating margin may provide a useful indicator of short-term performance — current period sales and manufacturing efficiency — and the successes from the development expenditures can be monitored with other forms of control, such as preaction reviews of expenditure proposals and monitoring of accomplishments against predefined milestones.[65]

The major problem with this operating-performance–isolation approach is that no clean distinction exists between operating expenditures and development expenditures. For example, manufacturing process improvements and market development programs will probably provide benefits (cost reductions or additional revenues) in the current *and* following periods, and managers will have some latitude to incur expenses either "above" or "below" the operating margin line. Thus, while operating margin may provide a better indicator of short-term success than does total income, it is still flawed.

Some companies use a variation of this approach in that they do not charge some operating units at all for some development expenses that benefit them. Corning Glass, General Electric, and Emerson Electric are among the companies that fund some types of business development at high (such as, division, corporate) organization levels until the investments begin to generate revenues in order to cushion department earnings from the impact of the expense.

Use of Nonfinancial Performance Measures

Many firms hold managers accountable for results areas that are defined in non-accounting terms, such as market share, number of patents granted, or sales generated from newly developed products. These performance indicators often make up a significant portion of management-by-objectives systems. For example, Xerox Corporation uses what it calls "competitive benchmarking." Managers of each function within each operating unit have to describe how Xerox products compare with those of Xerox's best competitors in terms of cost, quality, and product reliability. Then they have to develop a plan to attain competitive parity or superiority and sustain that position of leadership.[66]

Another example is the Metropolitan Division of Chemical Bank, which abandoned income statements for control of retail branches. Management decided that branch income statements were not very meaningful because some of the large items, such as interest income, varied directly with interest rates and were therefore largely uncontrollable. They replaced the income statements with a set of mostly nonfinancial performance indicators, such as growth in deposits, growth in number of accounts, and cost control, which were aggregated into an overall measure of performance according to a predetermined weighting scheme. The weights are adjusted as economic conditions or competitive or regulatory pressures change.

A third example is Emerson Electric, a company known for such strong financial controls that a 25-year unbroken string of record earnings has been produced. Emerson has recently changed its compensation system for division managers to lower the emphasis on bottom-line results. Ten percent of the company's division managers' bonuses are provided if plants are kept union free and 10–15 percent are provided if new products are developed. The company has also started to fund some development expenditures at the corporate level so as to cushion division earnings; the results of that effort have been good. Some promising new products have been developed, and one division president observed: "Under the pressure of quarterly earnings, [such products] wouldn't have been developed."[67]

While use of these nonfinancial measures provides a way of avoiding the measurement problems of FAC, this approach is not always a viable solution. The most significant limitation is the fact that it is often difficult to choose nonfinancial measures that are good indicators of economic income. In general, the choice is only easy when knowledge about the business strategy is relatively certain and detailed. Without a concrete strategy in mind, it is virtually impossible to know when good indicators of economic income have been chosen.

Another potential problem is that the performance indicators may not be stable. Just as strategies must adapt to changing environmental conditions, so must the nonfinancial performance indicators. If they are not changed in the face of changing environmental conditions, displacement will be the result.

A third problem is that it is difficult to choose the proper weighting among the items on a list of performance indicators. For example, if managers are to be held accountable for market share, cost control, and development of subordinates, they must be provided some guidance as to how those sometimes-conflicting goals should be balanced against each other. That is one of the real advantages of FAC; all goals are expressed in terms of one dimension: units of money (or purchasing power).

Use of Subjective Assessments of Performance

Because of the difficulty in selecting meaningful performance indicators that can be measured effectively, many managers rely on making subjective assessments of performance. That is, the managers make a personal evaluation of the results that have been achieved, possibly relying partially on objective performance indicators.

Subjective assessment also has drawbacks. One problem is that it is virtually impossible for an evaluator who has knowledge of the results that have been achieved to judge fairly what could have been achieved in the circumstances that were faced. Knowledge that an outcome has occurred generally increases its perceived *prior* probability of occurrence, and vice versa. In the psychology literature, this is known as "hindsight bias."[68] Hindsight bias is a particularly dangerous problem for subjective assessments of performance because it is an innate human limitation, and it can have a significant effect on the evaluations since, as many authors have observed its existence is generally not recognized: "Making sense of what one is told about the past seems so natural and effortless a response that one may be unaware that outcome knowledge has had any effect at all on him."[69]

There are also other potential problems. Subjective assessments of performance may be distorted by political considerations. And even if politics does not play a part in the evaluations, those whose performances are being evaluated may feel that the evaluations are not "fair." For example, consider the comments of a middle-level manager in a firm that had recently implemented a formula-based bonus system to replace a subjective assignment of bonuses:

> We used to have [subjective assignment of] bonuses here and the reason we're not doing that now . . . is that it always ended up in a war. They only had so much money to divvy up, and individual managers had preferences for their people. For an outstanding performance it wasn't so bad, but as soon as you got away from there and started awarding to people who had done just a good job, not a terribly great job, then it got into a real shoving match.[70]

This is not an unusual reaction.

These three problems — hindsight bias, political bias, and perceptions of unfairness — are possible, even likely, in virtually every situation in which subjective assessments of performances are used. Thus, while subjective assessment seems to be a way to avoid the measurement problems of results control, it adds other problems; it is not a panacea.

Emphasize Action and/or Personnel Controls

In most companies (and in some entities within each company) results control is not adequate by itself; it must be supplemented, or replaced, with other forms of control. The chief executive of a $2 billion corporation was quoted as saying:

> We can't just sit back and watch the numbers. We've got to know what the real issues are out there in the profit centers. Otherwise, we're not even in a position to check our managers on the big decisions.[71]

What he is suggesting is that he needs (or wants) to be in a position to use action controls, probably in the form of preaction reviews of at least the major decisions.

Most companies do use some action controls over even high-level general managers. This often takes the form of preaction reviews of plans, prospective employee hires, and investment proposals by top managers or their staff representatives. It can also take the form of centralization of certain key decisions — a form of behavioral constraint.

Some critics have suggested that most results controls should be replaced by action controls. One author suggested that the best form of control is a combination of personnel and action control, which he called "management by decisions."[72] The recommendation was that decision makers should be required to produce a "decision packet" that summarizes the problem or opportunity and the decision made. Superiors could then review some decision packets to ensure that decisions were being made properly and to assess the decision maker's "creativity, thoroughness, imagination, ability to analyze and evaluate situations, and judgment." This is a unique suggestion for a type of action accountability control, but its costs and the hindsight biases it would bring into play leave room for concern.

Action controls tend to dominate in centralized companies, such as smaller organizations, where top management possesses both detailed knowledge of the activities of the operating units and the time to monitor those activities carefully. But it is also used in large, decentralized companies that have relatively frequent reviews of management activities and performance and use elaborate staff organizations to monitor managerial actions.

Some other firms emphasize cultural control, such as through the creation of what Thomas Peters and Robert Waterman call "a homogeneous staff."[73] This is a form of personnel control that was discussed earlier.

CONCLUSION

This long chapter has been devoted to a discussion of the advantages and disadvantages of financial accountability controls. Because of its significant advantages, FAC has been the dominant form of control of managers for many years in large business organizations, particularly in the United States.

But many recent articles have been critical of FAC. Much of this criticism has been stimulated by the apparent difficulty of U.S. businesses to compete with Japanese businesses, in particular, which rely on forms of control that are not highly oriented toward FAC. This has brought about a period of questioning, experimentation, and change. While it is recognized that FAC still has some significant advantages, many people have blamed it for several serious types of problems, including management myopia, excessive risk aversion, and gamesmanship.

The trend, however, seems not to be toward Japanese management styles; rather, it seems to be toward an increasing emphasis on results controls at managerial levels in business organizations, both in the United States and Europe. For example, the summary of the annual survey of executive compensation practices conducted by *Financial Executive* noted a trend toward a greater portion of executive pay being derived from "variable components which are performance based," and this trend was expected to continue.[74] Similarly, *Business Week* reported that "the boards of virtually every major U.S. corporation are exploring ways to link executive pay more closely to shareholders' interests."[75]

This same trend seems to be taking place in European business firms, although at a much slower pace. In Europe, firms have traditionally relied heavily on intangible rewards (for example, job security) that are not explicitly linked to performance. But the larger firms seem to be moving toward greater use of monetary incentives for good results. The comment of Heinz Durr, chief executive of AEG-Telefunken, a large West German firm, is not unusual: "You can't run a decentralized company without results–related compensation."[76]

This necessarily leads back to consideration of the problems that use of FAC seems to generate. To take advantage of the benefits of FAC while minimizing the problems, firms have tried a number of solutions. Some of these solutions involve alterations to the historical cost-accounting measures of performance on which FAC is typically based. Some involve other measurement alternatives such as inflation accounting. Some involve value-based measures of performance based on stock price changes or estimates of changes in future cash flow potentials. And some involve supplementation or replacement of FAC with one or more forms of action or personnel controls.

The key to solution, or at least alleviation, of many of the harmful side effects is recognition of the fact that FAC based on historical cost-accounting measures of performance has some significant drawbacks. This chapter discussed a number of FAC modifications or alternatives that might be considered, but each of these alternatives has its own advantages and disadvantages. Which alternatives will prove over time to provide the best results in which situations is still an open question.

The incompleteness aspect of FAC seems not to be the major problem. It is true that FAC measures are not complete since it is not possible to express all desirable results in financial terms, but this is a well-recognized problem. The other desirable results (such as, responsibility to employees and society) must be controlled in some other way.

NOTES

1. A recent survey of 620 medium-to-large-size corporations (>$90 million annual sales) found that fewer than 5 percent had neither profit nor investment centers. James S. Reece and William R. Cool, "Measuring Investment Center Performance," *Harvard Business Review* 56 (May-June 1978): 28–49.

2. For example, see Louis J. Brindisi, "Executive Compensation Programs Go Wrong," *Wall Street Journal,* June 14, 1982, p. 20; Mark C. Ubelhart, "A New Look at Executive Compensation Plans," *Cashflow* 2 (May 1981): 20–24.

3. See, for example, Edwin S. Mruk and James A. Giardina, "Executive Compensation Tenth Edition Study," *Financial Executive* (October 1982): 49–55.

4. Lester C. Thurow, "Where Management Fails," *Newsweek,* December 7, 1981, p. 78.

5. Robert H. Hayes and William J. Abernathy, "Managing Our Way to Economic Decline," *Harvard Business Review* 58 (July-August 1980): 70.

6. Kenneth L. Block, chairman of the A. T. Kearney consulting firm, quoted in D. O. Cloninger, "American Myopia," *Collegiate Forum* (Fall 1981): 6.

7. "What's Wrong with Management," *Dun's Business Month* 119 (April 1982): 48.

8. Hayes and Abernathy, "Managing," p. 70.

9. Lisa Miller Mesdag, "The 50 Largest Private Industrial Companies," *Fortune,* May 31, 1982, p. 111.

10. William C. Norris, "How to Expand R & D Cooperation," *Business Week,* April 11, 1983, p. 21.

11. "Listening to the Voice of the Marketplace," *Business Week,* February 21, 1983, p. 90.

12. See, for example, Jack L. Treynor, "The Financial Objective in the Widely Held Corporation," *Financial Analysts Journal* 37 (March-April 1981): 68–71; and Allen H. Seed III, "New Approaches to Asset Management," *Journal of Business Strategy* 3 (Winter 1983): 16–22.

13. Financial Accounting Standards Board, *Financial Reporting and Changing Prices: Statement of Accounting Standards no. 33* (Stamford, Conn.: Financial Accounting Standards Board, 1979), p. 65.

14. As examples of strong criticisms of return on investments of performance, in particular, see Stanley Henrici, "The Perversity, Peril and Pathos of ROI," *Financial Analysts Journal* 39 (September-October 1983): 79–80; and John Dearden, "The Case against ROI Control," *Harvard Business Review* XLVII (May-June 1969): 124–35.

15. William H. Beaver, *Financial Reporting: An Accounting Revolution* (Englewood Cliffs, N.J.: Prentice-Hall, 1981).

16. Alfred Rappaport, "Selecting Strategies That Create Shareholder Value," *Harvard Business Review* 59 (May-June 1981): 139–49.

17. Ezra Solomon and J. C. Laya, "Measurement of Company Profitability: Some Systematic Errors in the Accounting Rate of Return," in *Financial Research and Management Decisions,* ed. Alexander A. Robickek (New York: Wiley, 1967), pp. 152–79.

18. Financial Accounting Standards Board, *Accounting for Research and Development Costs: Statement of Financial Accounting Standards no. 2* (Stamford, Conn.: Financial Accounting Standards Board, 1974).
19. For example, see Bertrand N. Horwitz and Richard Kolodny, "The Economic Effects of Involuntary Uniformity in the Financial Reporting of R & D Expenditures," *Journal of Accounting Research* (supp. 1980): 38–74.
20. Michael Chatfield, *A History of Accounting Thought* (Hinsdale, Ill.: Dryden, 1974).
21. Richard P. Brief, "The Origin and Evolution of Nineteenth-Century Asset Accounting," *Business History Review* XL (1966): 1–2.
22. For example, see Robert S. Kaplan, *Advanced Management Accounting* (Englewood Cliffs, N.J.: Prentice-Hall, 1981).
23. See, for example, "Executives Keep Reducing the Risks of a High-Reward Career," *Business Week,* May 9, 1983, p. 83.
24. Not all managers behave in a risk-averse fashion all the time. Examples of managers who have been successful largely because of their abilities to take prudent risks include Victor Posner (Miami financier) and Jack Welch (chairman of General Electric Company).
25. Personal interview with a general manager in a large, diversified firm.
26. "Did Warner-Lambert Make a $468 Million Mistake?" *Business Week,* November 21, 1983, p. 123.
27. Example provided by Richard F. Vancil.
28. Personal interview with a general manager in a large, diversified firm.
29. Kenneth A. Merchant, "The Effects of Organizational Controls" (Working Paper, Graduate School of Business Administration, Harvard University, 1984).
30. For example, virtually every issue of *Forbes* magazine includes an article under the heading "Numbers Game." Many of these articles criticize either the precision or the objectivity of accounting numbers, or both.
31. For example, there should be no debate as to how to account for a cash sale.
32. George J. Staubus, *Making Accounting Decisions* (Houston, Tex.: Scholars, 1977), p. 206.
33. For example, see Abraham J. Briloff, *Unaccountable Accounting* (New York: Harper & Row, 1972); "Cooking the Books," *Dun's Business Month* 120 (January 1983): 40; and George Getschow, "Slick Accounting Ploys Help Many Companies Improve Their Income," *Wall Street Journal,* June 20, 1980, p. 1.
34. See, for example, Richard L. Hudson, "SEC Charges Fudging of Corporate Figures Is a Growing Practice," *Wall Street Journal,* June 2, 1983, p. 1.
35. Personal interview with a general manager in a large electronics firm.
36. See, for example, Zvi Bodie, " 'Compound-Interest' Depreciation in Capital Investment," *Harvard Business Review* 60 (May-June 1982): 58–60.
37. "Capital Offense," *Forbes,* January 17, 1983, pp. 100–101; also see Jan Johnson, "Comserv Does Its Books," *Datamation* 29 (December 1983): 55–66.
38. "SEC Halts Spread of Accounting Method That Increases Profit of Software Firms," *Wall Street Journal,* April 15, 1983, p. 10.
39. See, for example, Frank J. Fabozzi and Robert Fonfeder, "Have You Seen Any

Good Quarterly Statements Lately?" *Journal of Portfolio Management* 9 (Winter 1983): 71–74.

40. Alfred Rappaport, "Corporate Performance Standards and Shareholder Value," *Journal of Business Strategy* 3 (Spring 1983): 28–38.
41. David F. Larcker, "The Association between Performance Plan Adoption and Corporate Capital Investment," *Journal of Accounting and Economics* 5 (1983): 3–30.
42. Personal interview with the financial vice-president of a large, diversified corporation.
43. Personal interviews.
44. Carol J. Loomis, "How GE Manages Inflation," *Fortune,* May 4, 1981, pp. 121–24.
45. Kenneth R. Todd, Jr., "How One Financial Officer Uses Inflation-Adjusted Accounting Data," *Financial Executive* 50 (October 1982): 13–19.
46. Geoffrey Smith, "Hard Choices, the Hard Way," *Forbes,* November 7, 1983, p. 108.
47. "TRW Leads a Revolution in Managing Technology," *Business Week,* November 15, 1982, p. 124.
48. John L. Grant, "Inflation's Full Impact on the Bottom Line," *Business Week,* February 7, 1983, p. 8.
49. Charles T. Horngren, "Inflation and Internal Accounting," in *Current Cost Accounting, Its Aspects and Impacts: Proceedings of April 1983 Conference,* chap. 9 (Dallas: Center for International Accounting Development, University of Texas at Dallas, 1983).
50. Financial Accounting Standards Board, *Financial Reporting and Changing Prices.*
51. See, for example, J. Edward Ketz, "Are Constant Dollar Disclosures Informative?" *Financial Analysts Journal* 39 (March–April 1983): 52–55; William H. Beaver, Paul A. Griffin, and Wayne R. Landsman, "The Incremental Information Content of Replacement Cost Earnings," *Journal of Accounting and Economics* 4 (1982): 15–39; and William H. Beaver and Wayne R. Landsman, *Incremental Information Content of Statement 33 Disclosures* (Stamford, Conn.: Financial Accounting Standards Board, 1983).
52. For example, see Eric Flamholtz, *Human Resource Accounting* (Encino, Calif.: Dickinson, 1974).
53. Alfred Rappaport, "Selecting Strategies," pp. 139–49.
54. Securities and Exchange Commission, "Adoption of Requirements for Financial Accounting and Reporting Practices for Oil and Gas Producing Activities," Accounting Series Release no. 253, August 31, 1978; and Securities and Exchange Commission, "Oil and Gas Producers — Supplemental Disclosures on the Basis of Reserve Recognition Accounting," Accounting Series Release no. 269, September 24, 1979.
55. RRA-type disclosures are still required of oil and gas producing companies in annual financial statements.
56. See, for example, C. Wayne Alderman, Glenn E. Summers, and Mary Jeanne Welsh, "The Trend toward Soft Data in Accounting," *Management Accounting* LXV (December 1983): 34–39.

57. For example, see Kenneth A. Merchant and William J. Bruns, Jr., "Measure Better, Manage Better: A Cure for Management Myopia" (Working Paper no. 83–83, Graduate School of Business Administration, Harvard University, 1983); and Rappaport, "Corporate Performance Standards and Shareholder Value," pp. 28–38.

58. Personal interview with a planning manager in a large manufacturing and distribution firm.

59. Jeffrey M. Traynor and Kenneth A. Merchant, "Natomas North America (C)," case no. 9–184–033 (Boston: HBS Case Services, 1983).

60. See, for example, Kenneth A. Merchant, "ES, Inc.," case no. 9–183–061 (Boston: HBS Case Services, 1982).

61. Robert S. Kaplan, "Measuring Manufacturing Performance: A New Challenge for Managerial Accounting Research," *Accounting Review* LVIII (October 1983): 686–705.

62. "Prime Computer Sees Net Down in 2nd Period But Up for Full Year," *Wall Street Journal,* May 18, 1983, p. 20.

63. Erik Larson and Carrie Dolan, "Once All Alone in Field, Apple Computer Girds for Industry Shakeout," *Wall Street Journal,* October 4, 1983, p. 1.

64. "How Signode's Managers Turned into Entrepreneurs," *Business Week,* June 6, 1983, p. 86.

65. A more complete discussion of this approach is presented in Richard F. Vancil, "Better Management of Corporate Development," *Harvard Business Review* 50 (September-October 1972): 53–62.

66. "Letter to Shareholders," Xerox Corporation, 1982 Annual Report.

67. "Emerson Electric: High Profits from Low Tech," *Business Week,* April 4, 1983, p. 58.

68. See, for example, Baruch Fischhoff, "Hindsight/Foresight: The Effect of Outcome Knowledge on Judgment under Uncertainty," *Journal of Experimental Psychology: Human Perception and Performance* 1 (May 1975): 288–99; and Baruch Fischhoff and Ruth Beyth, " 'I Knew It Would Happen — Remembered Probabilities of Once-Future Things," *Organizational Behavior and Human Performance* 13 (February 1975): 1–16.

69. Fischhoff, "Hindsight/Foresight," p. 298.

70. Interview with a middle manager in a medium-sized electronics firm.

71. Carter F. Bales, "Strategic Control: The President's Paradox," *Business Horizons* 20 (August 1977): 17–28.

72. Charles H. Ford, "Manage by Decisions, Not by Objectives," *Business Horizons* 23 (February 1980): 7–18. Similar suggestions were made by Gary B. Brumback, "Revisiting an Approach to Managing Behaviors and Results," *Public Personnel Management Journal* 10 (Summer 1981): 270–77.

73. Thomas J. Peters and Robert H. Waterman, *In Search of Excellence* (New York: Harper & Row, 1982), p. 290.

74. Edwin S. Mruk and James A. Giardina, "Executive Compensation: Eleventh Edition Study," *Financial Executive* LI (October 1983): 42.

75. "Turnover at the Top," *Business Week,* December 19, 1983, p. 106; also see Carol J. Loomis, "The Madness of Executive Compensation," *Fortune,* July 12, 1982, pp. 42–52.

76. "Europe's New Managers: Going Global with a U.S. Style," *Business Week,* May 24, 1982, p. 116.

chapter nine

CONTROL SYSTEM DESIGN

The preceding chapters have outlined a framework that is useful for understanding the controls that can be used in organizations and how they affect behaviors, both positively and negatively. This chapter explores how this framework can be used by those who are interested in designing control systems or in analyzing existing systems. Both of these processes — design or analysis — require addressing two basic questions: What controls should be used? and How tightly should each be applied? The answers to these questions are not easy; they depend on understanding what it is that is being controlled *and* how the individuals affected will react to the controls that are implemented. The following sections describe how the information to answer these questions can be structured, and the chapter concludes with some observations about common control issues.

NECESSITY OF ACQUIRING SOME UNDERSTANDING OF THE SITUATION

A conscious attempt to answer the two key control questions — what controls to use and how tightly to apply them — depends on recognizing or developing two important pieces of information. The first is an understanding of the roles being controlled: that is, what it is that the organization wants the individuals involved to do. The second is about why it might be possible that the desired actions will not be achieved (that is, what control problems might exist). Because these two pieces of information are so important, it is useful to discuss in some detail how they might be uncovered and/or developed.

Understanding Role Demands

Assembling knowledge about what the involved individuals should do is a necessary first step to being able to design a system of controls or to analyze the effectiveness of one that is in place. And the more knowledge the better, because greater and more certain knowledge yields a larger set of feasible control alternatives, provides a better chance of being able to apply each alternative tightly, if so desired, and reduces the chances of creating a behavioral displacement problem. This understanding is most valuable if it is defined in terms of the actions desired, since the purpose of controls is to influence actions, but controls can be devised with only an understanding of some desirable results or personnel characteristics.

Objectives and strategies often provide important guides to the actions that are expected, and they are more valuable if they are understood well enough that they can be described with at least some minimal level of specificity. For example, a nonspecific statement of objectives — such as "the objective of ABC Corporation is to serve the long-term interests of its shareholders, its employees, and society" — provides only general guidance as to what employees in the firm should do. It is possible to determine that some actions will not serve any of these interests, but that knowledge is not as useful as knowing how the trade-offs between conflicting objectives should be handled. To provide further guidance as to what is required, firms often set performance constraints such as, "We are seeking a 15 percent return on invested capital after taxes and a 20 percent growth in sales."[1]

Specifying the strategies to be followed is another way to guide behaviors; and like objectives, strategies can be expressed in vague or specific terms. For example, having a business unit employ a "growth strategy" is less specific than detailing how the growth should be accomplished (for example, what market segments to emphasize) and how the growth-versus-current returns trade-offs should be made. For control purposes, more specific objectives and strategies are preferable, assuming they are congruent with true organizational goals and can be updated so as to be kept congruent.

Knowledge of what is desirable is most useful for control purposes if it can be translated into knowledge of the specific demands on the roles of individuals (or perhaps groups) in the organization. Much of this elaboration and translation is done as part of the organization's planning and budgeting processes. Role demands can be specified in terms of either the *key actions* that must be performed or the *key results* that determine success or failure in that role.

Understanding Role Demands in Terms of Key Actions

One way to understand what must be controlled is to identify the key actions (KAs) that must be performed in order to provide the greatest probability of success. These actions differ considerably among firms and among different roles in a firm.

It is not always easy to isolate a short list of KAs, but sometimes it can be done, particularly for the recurring actions, or what Drucker calls the "regular process."[2] For lower-level personnel, such as production line workers, the KAs may be well understood because they are highly routinized and largely mechanical, such as folding a garment and placing it in a box. For a professional service firm, the KAs may be the hiring decisions; a manager in such a firm noted:

> One of the major tools, if not *the* major tool, that we have in achieving our goals is through control of the number and quality of the people we hire.[3]

But most KAs for most higher-level line personnel (that is, managers), are not well understood. They may include problem finding, personnel team building, and investment decision making and these types of actions require considerable professional judgment, it is usually impossible to judge whether the actions taken are appropriate except through close monitoring by someone with equal or greater professional qualifications. Similarly, judgments of the effectiveness of the key recurring actions of higher-level staff professionals, such as market analysts, economists, or lawyers, can be made only by reviews by peers or superiors.

That is not to say that some KAs of higher-level personnel cannot be isolated for control purposes. Most companies require standard sets of actions for personnel preparing investment proposals, business plans, and justifications for new hires. These are action controls.

Understanding Role Demands in Terms of Key Results

Another way to understand role demands is in terms of the key results (KRs).[4] They can be defined as:

> the few key areas where "things must go right" for the business to flourish. If results in these areas are not adequate, the organization's efforts for the period will be less than desired.[5]

In most situations the number of KRs that must be considered is small, perhaps six or eight at most.[6] For example, the Ryder System, Inc., the largest truck-leasing and rental company in the United States, apparently seems to have only two KRs at the company level — utilization of assets and market share. Ryder's chairman observed that "if you put those two factors together, you end up increasing your profitability."[7] At different organization levels and within different functions with Ryder, however, the list may be longer. For the purchasing manager within Ryder to be effective, he or she would have to ensure the right quantity (and mix) of quality vehicles (and other items), on schedule and at reasonable cost.

KRs may or may not be stable. For some companies and entities within a company, the KRs may be relatively constant over time; for others they may change as the environmental conditions and/or the chosen strategy change. For example, a company that is pursuing a low-cost-producer strategy must monitor costs carefully, and if it is in a situation where costs are declining with cumulative experience (that is, there is a learning curve), it must maintain a strong market share position. These are KRs that are relatively constant. A switch to a different strategy — such as to market a unique, differentiated product — will change the KRs. Control of the individuals charged with carrying out this new strategy will probably require measurement product performance characteristics and comparing them with those of competitors, or implementation of action controls over the design efforts.

UNDERSTANDING WHAT CONTROL PROBLEMS MIGHT EXIST

The second part of the situational analysis involves considering why the KAs might not be taken or the KRs not accomplished. This is important because, as discussed in earlier chapters, the different types of controls are not equally effective at addressing each of the control problems. Table 9.1 provides a summary of the control problems each of the types of controls addresses. It shows, for example, that behavioral constraints do not help solve lack-of-direction problems; so if direction is a significant problem in the area of concern, other forms of controls will have to be considered.

DECISION 1: CHOICE OF CONTROLS

Only when this understanding of what needs to be controlled — the KAs or the KRs — and why they might not happen — the control problems — has

Table 9.1. Control Types and Control Problems

Controls	Lack of Direction	Motivational Problems	Personal Limitations
Results:			
Results accountability	X	X	
Actions:			
Behavioral constraints		X	
Preaction reviews	X	X	X
Action accountability	X	X	X
Redundancy			X
Personnel:			
Selection and placement	X	X	X
Training	X		X
Culture	X	X	
Group-based rewards	X	X	
Provision of necessary resources			X

been assembled can a control system be designed or analyzed. Then the questions as to what controls should be used and how tightly they should be applied can be addressed.

The specific set of control mechanisms to be selected from among the feasible alternatives should be those that will provide the greatest net benefits (that is, benefits less costs). The benefits of a control system are derived from the increased probability of success; but since controls are usually costly to implement and operate, these costs must be subtracted from the total benefits provided.

Personnel Controls as an Initial Consideration

In deciding among the many control alternatives, it is logical to start by considering if personnel controls will be sufficient. This is true because personnel controls usually have relatively few harmful side effects and relatively low out-of-pocket costs, and in some cases they may provide completely effective control by themselves, which is often the case for smaller businesses. Consider, for example, this observation by the chairman of a small high-technology start-up company in response to a question as to what control meant to his company:

We don't have a need for most of the controls that large companies have. We're still small — just three professionals and twenty people in our order-taking, assembly, and packing areas — and we're all working as hard as we can, some of us twelve to fourteen hours a day, seven days a week. We understand what we want to do, and we're highly motivated to do it. We don't have any bonus system, and the only budget we have is a simple cash forecast. I guess you could say the most important part of our control system is the information we collect, particularly about where the market is headed and how our products stack up against those of our competitors.[8]

This company obviously has little need for results or action controls at this stage of its evolution.

But even in settings in which they cannot be acceptably effective by themselves, it is useful to focus first on personnel controls, because personnel controls have to be relied on to some extent anyway; none of the control mechanisms that can be added will provide perfect control. One obvious place where this central importance of personnel control can be seen in most firms is in the area of allocations of scarce resources. Most allocations of scarce resources are based at least somewhat on the felt degree of trust in the individuals involved. This was one of the strong findings in a large study of decentralized organizations conducted by Richard Vancil,[9] and this aspect of management emerges consistently in interviews with managers. For example, this observation, made by a middle manager in a large U.S. firm that is generally recognized for its managerial excellence, is typical: "Getting money is a very personal process. Very few ideas get funded without good sponsorship."[10]

This same point about the central role of personnel control in firms was emphasized more generally by Don Johnston, chairman and chief executive of the JWT Group, parent company of the J. Walter Thompson advertising agency. His firm was hurt recently by a control system failure, and this experience led him to draw the following conclusion:

> As long as business depends on human beings, we will all be vulnerable to human frailty. . . . In today's world, you are more than ever dependent on the personal integrity of the people involved.[11]

Trust and other personnel controls will be sufficient, however, only if the people in the particular roles being considered (or those who might be put in the roles) understand what is required, are capable of performing well, and are motivated to perform well without additional rewards or punishments provided by the organization. Unfortunately, many examples are available to show that this is rarely the case.

Between 1976 and 1980 the president of a small candy distributorship relied on personnel controls while attempting to set up new businesses to diversify his operations. He hired people who he thought were experienced and trustworthy to run the new businesses, which included exporting, trucking, auto leasing, computer software development, and wine distribution. He was not concerned that he did not understand those businesses well nor the fact that his company did not have good financial-reporting systems. The results were disastrous. Four years later, none of the new businesses had survived; he was stuck with considerable excess inventory and the payables for them; and his business, which had been quite profitable up until that time, was in danger of failing.[12]

While this particular executive could be faulted for his implementation of personnel controls, (such as, one of his new employees turned out to be an alcoholic), it is rare that personnel controls are, by themselves, sufficient. In most cases it is necessary to supplement them with controls over actions, results, or both, as one of the most commonly cited principles of control is: "You shouldn't put all your trust in one person."[13]

The choice between action and results controls should depend on the particular advantages and disadvantages each has in the setting in question. These are discussed in the following sections.

The Advantages and Disadvantages of Action Controls

Perhaps the most significant advantage of action controls is that where they are feasible, they are the most direct form of control. If it is absolutely essential that an action be performed properly the first time (for example, a significant loan decision in a bank), action controls usually provide the best control because the control-action link is so direct. If controls over the actions themselves are judged to be adequate, there is no need to monitor results.

Action controls also provide several other advantages. One is that they direct managerial attention to the actions being used within the firm. Debates and conflicts that arise will then be focused on the right questions.

Action controls also tend to lead to documentation of the accumulation of knowledge as to what works best. The documents that are produced (for example, policies and procedures) are an efficient way to transfer accumulations of knowledge to the people who are performing the actions. They also act as a form of organizational memory, so that the knowledge is not lost if, for example, key employees leave the organization.

Finally, action controls, particularly in the form of policies and procedures, are an efficient way to aid organizational coordination. They increase the predictability of actions and reduce the amount of interorganizational information flows required to achieve a coordinated effort. They are a key element in a *bureaucratic* form of organization (using this term in a positive sense) which makes the organization "capable of attaining the highest degree of efficiency and is in this the most rational known means of carrying out the imperative of control over human beings."[14]

But action controls have a number of significant disadvantages. One is a severe feasibility limitation. As discussed earlier, excellent knowledge of what actions are desirable exists only for highly routinized jobs.

Second, most forms of action controls discourage creativity, innovation, and adaptation. Most people react to action controls by developing their habits around following the rules, and this adaptation may be so complete that they begin to depend on the rules, cease to think how the processes could be improved, and become very resistant to change. An apt title for this phenomenon is "bureaupathic behavior."[15] In some cases this discouragement is not a significant disadvantage — for example, creativity from pilots in the air is not normally desirable. But in other cases, action controls cause significant opportunities for improvements to be foregone.

A third disadvantage of action controls is that some, perhaps even most, people are not happy operating under them. Some people, especially the more independent, creative people, may leave to find other jobs that allow more opportunity for achievement and self-actualization.

A fourth disadvantage, of action accountability in particular, is that congruence is a serious concern. It is easy to focus on actions of lesser importance that are easy to monitor. Furthermore, it is difficult and costly to adapt procedures to changing environments. As noted in a recent book:

> It has long since become a familiar observation that generals regularly spend their time preparing to fight the previous war. Managers often do the same. Whether from the force of habit or from the appeal of comfortable modes of thought and action, they often fail to see how the problems that beset them are unlike those with which they have become familiar. Or they fail to make the painful effort to determine what from the past continues to apply, what does not, and that what is new must be learned.[16]

Indeed, most companies have difficulty in modifying their procedures as situations change, and communicating changes that are made can be very expensive. Several of the problems that were discussed in Chapter 7 (for example, the tendency toward bureaucratization of behavior) were caused by procedures that did not adapt to changing conditions.

A final disadvantage of action controls is that where the actions being controlled require professional judgment, action control is difficult and costly. The monitoring or after-the-fact evaluations of the actions taken must be done by individuals who are as well or more qualified than those who are making the judgments being controlled. These people are highly skilled and well paid, and they are typically not highly motivated to perform these review or audit functions. As a consequence, where other control alternatives exist for professionals, action controls are usually used sparingly.

The Advantages and Disadvantages of Results Controls

Results controls also have several significant advantages and disadvantages. One advantage is feasibility. Results controls can provide effective control even where knowledge as to what actions are desirable is lacking. This situation is typical of many (even most) of the important roles in many organizations.

Another advantage is that peoples' behaviors can be influenced even while they are allowed significant autonomy. This is particularly desirable where creativity is required because autonomy allows room for new and innovative ways of thinking. But even where creativity is not important, allowing autonomy has some advantages. It usually yields greater employee commitment and motivation because higher-level personal needs (such as, for personal accomplishment) are brought into play. It can provide on-the-job training, as people learn by doing and by making mistakes. It also allows room for idiosyncratic styles of behavior (for example, a unique sales approach), which can provide better results than standardization of an approach.

A final advantage of results controls is that they are often inexpensive. Performance measures are often collected for reasons not directly related to management control, such as for financial reporting, tax reporting, or strategy formulation, and if these measures can be used or easily adapted for results control use, the incremental expense of the control can be relatively small.

Results controls, however, have two major disadvantages. First, results measures often provide poor indicators of whether good actions had been taken, because the measures failed to meet one or more of the qualities of good measures — congruence, precision, objectivity, timeliness, or understandability — or because the results were influenced by factors over which the person involved had little control. As discussed earlier, it is often difficult to fix these measurement problems, and even to recognize that they exist.

The second problem is that results targets are often asked to perform two important, but competing, control functions. The first is motivation to achieve. For this function it is best for the targets to be challenging but achievable.[17] The other function is communication. Plans are often treated as commitments and passed among the various entities in an organization so that each entity knows what to expect from the other entities. For this function the targets should be a best guess, or maybe even slightly conservative, to make sure they are achieved. Obviously, one set of plans cannot serve both purposes optimally; one purpose (or both) must be sacrificed if results controls are used.

DECISION 2: TIGHT VERSUS LOOSE CONTROL

The decision as to whether controls should be tight or loose in any particular company, or area within the company, depends on the answers to three questions. First, What are the potential benefits? Is the area being considered important to the firm, and are one or more of the control problems likely to cause harm? Tight control is most beneficial over the critical areas of the company.

Second, Are any harmful side effects likely? If all the conditions necessary to make a type of control feasible, such as knowledge about how the control object relates to the desired ends, are not present, harmful side effects are likely if the control is implemented; this is particularly true if the control is implemented in tight form. For example, if the environment is very unpredictable and the need for creativity high, such as is the case for high-technology firms, good knowledge does not exist about either the actions that are needed or the results that should be accomplished. Therefore, neither action nor results control can be said to be clearly feasible, and the implementation of either in tight form is likely to cause problems. Tight action controls would likely cause behavioral displacement and tend to stifle creativity; tight results controls would limit adaptability, as results standards are often very difficult to adjust to the changing environmental conditions.

Third, What are the costs involved in implementing tight controls? Some forms of control are very costly to implement in tight form. Tight action controls in the form of preaction reviews, for example, can require considerable top management time. Tight results controls might require extensive studies to gather useful performance standards, or they might require new information systems or measuring equipment.

In a recent best-selling book, Peters and Waterman observed that a number of companies that they defined as "excellent" employ what they call "simultaneous tight-loose controls."[18] They observed that the control systems used in these companies can be considered *loose* in that they allow — and even encourage — autonomy, entrepreneurship, and innovation but that these same control systems can also be called *tight* because the people in the company share a set of rigid values (such as, focus on customers' needs). Peters and Waterman observed that policies and procedures and other types of controls are not necessary in these companies because "people way down the line know what they are supposed to do in most situations because the handful of guiding values is crystal clear"[19] and "culture regulates rigorously the few variables that do count."[20] In other words, in the terminology used in this book, the control systems in these companies are dominated by *personnel (cultural) control*.

It sounds like nirvana: Let culture provide a high degree of reliance that the firms' employees are acting in its best interest and avoid most of the harmful side effects. But this desirable state is very difficult to achieve, and Peters and Waterman's observations do not provide much useful advice for managers of companies whose employees do not share a set of rigidly shared values.[21] And these companies without strong cultures seem to be far in the majority.[22] What do these managers do?

It may be possible to approach a similar type of simultaneous tight-loose control even where a strong culture does not exist. This can be accomplished by using tight controls over the few key factors, either actions or results, that have the greatest potential impact on the success of the organization. More control should be exercised over strategically important areas than over minor areas, regardless of how easy it is to control each. Every KA or KR area should be controlled as tightly as possible because failure in one of these areas is, by definition, very costly. None of the controls that might be substituted for culture can be assumed to be free of harmful side effects, but selective use of tight controls may limit these effects. Most individuals can probably tolerate a few restrictions if they are allowed some freedom of action in other areas.

THE ADVANTAGES OF USING MULTIPLE FORMS OF CONTROL

In many situations it is beneficial to use more than one form of control. One advantage of multiple forms of control is that if they are needed and if they are well designed, they should provide better control. They can reinforce each other, and they can address a broader set of control problems.

Another advantage is that the use of multiple forms of control provides possibilities for *learning*, in particular, how actions or certain personnel characteristics are related to results. This information can be useful in improving the controls at a later time. There is a danger that this type of feedback may be distorted, however, because it is impossible to see the results of actions not taken.

The only drawbacks to the use of multiple forms of control are cost and the increased possibility of dysfunctional side effects. These can be very significant, of course.

CONTROL NEEDS AND FEASIBLE ALTERNATIVES CHANGE OVER TIME

That is not to say that one form of control cannot be emphasized, however. In fact, most firms do emphasize one form of control, and they often change their emphasis from one form to another as their needs and capabilities change. For example, as has been noted often, small companies can often be controlled adequately through the supervisory ability of a strong owner-manager, but as the companies grow, this form of action control has to be replaced. Here is an observation about that point specifically referring to control in developing chains of restaurants:

> Energetic entrepreneurs are often very successful competitors because of their ability to control operations through intensive personal supervision of all the details of the restaurant. As the firm expands and the volume of business and number of locations increase, the task of control quickly exceeds the abilities of even the best entrepreneurial manager.[23]

As a consequence, as firms grow their controls evolve, usually toward increased formalization of procedures for action accountability purposes and/or development of more elaborate information systems for results control purposes.[24]

This progression away from centralization and action control can be observed in many companies. It occurred at the Massachusetts Port Authority (Massport). From 1963 to 1974 the control system at Massport was dominated by personnel and action controls. The executive director, Ed King, was a strong leader who developed a staff of loyal employees, but he also centralized many key decisions and involved himself personally in detailed reviews of budgets and expenditures. King's successor, David Davis, instead chose to implement a formal decentralized control system with the emphasis on "clear responsibility and accountability at the operational levels."[25]

Had he remained in the organization as it grew, King might also have had to implement more formal controls, but much of the difference in approaches to control must be attributed to differences in management style. The important point is that it is not possible to say that one control system worked better than the other.

KEEPING A BEHAVIORAL FOCUS

What makes the analysis of controls so difficult is that the benefits and the side effects of each of the controls are dependent on how people will react to the controls that are being considered, and predicting behaviors is far from an exact science. Regardless of the difficulty, it is important to maintain this behavioral focus because the benefits of controls are derived only from their impacts on behaviors.

To illustrate the difficulty in predicting reactions to controls, consider the motivation issue. Use of accountability controls is based on the assumption that behavior can be influenced by providing rewards (or punishments) for certain aspects of performance, and it does appear that rewards (and punishments) are effective in affecting most individuals' motivations; these effects are apparent even across economic systems and cultures. The Soviet Union recently acted on this assumption about motivation and instituted a new program of "discipline" to "weed out" corruption, absenteeism, sloppy work, and alcoholism. This program increases both the rewards (particularly pay) for good work and the penalties for bad behaviors, such as in the form of withholding of vacations, loss of job, or jail.[26] Similarly, the People's Republic of China is moving away from centralization of production and distribution in favor of a "responsibility system," which allows the personnel in factories, farms, and other economic units to share in the profits of improved efficiency and innovation.[27]

But some people may not respond as expected. For example, promising money for good performance may not be effective, perhaps, because the individuals involved are already highly motivated for other reasons (for example, peer pressure), because they already have enough money, or because the after-tax benefit is not worth the additional effort or risk.[28]

Despite some similarities among the assumptions made about behaviors by managers operating in different cultures, such as the ones noted above, cultural differences seem to explain many differences in how people respond to different rewards *and* why particular management practices are used. A summary quotation from a cross-cultural management study explains:

> Motivational needs in Norway are more dependent on good colleague relationships than in the U.S. Denmark and the U.S. have a much more individual orientation to motivation than Norway. "Promotion" is a motivational criteria [*sic*] in the U.S. but not in the Scandinavian countries. Leadership in Norway is more socially oriented than in Germany. Decision-making analysis shows more individuality within a group in Norway than in the Anglo-Saxon countries. Thus, it is not only impossible to use a universal theory of management for all types of businesses, but it becomes apparent that cultural differences make it even more irrelevant.[29]

Another huge, culturally oriented study — of 88,000 employees of a multinational corporation located in 67 countries — offered similar conclusions that organizations are culture bound and that theories of how people will respond to various types of controls must be adapted to the culture.[30]

Similar behavioral differences also exist among people in different parts of a single country, in different firms, and in different areas of the same firm, and managers must be aware of such differences because the effectiveness of the controls used will vary depending on the reactions of the people involved. For example, "creative types" such as advertising executives and design engineers tend to react more negatively to action controls than do persons working in accounting or personnel. And some employees, particularly those at lower organizational levels, seem to be relatively highly interested in money as a reward, whereas others are more interested in stimulating work, autonomy, and challenge.[31]

These differences make the application of controls particularly challenging, and it is crucial to emphasize that there is no one best form of control; what works best in one company, or area within a company, may not work in another. However, it is still important to keep the focus on the *people* involved because it is their responses that will determine the success or failure of the control system.

THE UNDESIRABLE STATE OF BEING "OUT OF CONTROL"

As a way of concluding, it is useful to consider what causes companies to have control problems so serious that the company is labeled as being "out of control." Actually, this condition is not rare. The list of companies that have been criticized for poor controls in recent years includes Warner Communications,[32] Verbatim,[33] Rockwell International,[34] Mattel,[35] Chemical Investors,[36] Fairchild Camera and Instrument (before the takeover by Schlumberger),[37] and Tandem.[38]

The causes of the problems these companies have had can probably all be described in terms of (1) an imperfect understanding of the setting and/or the effect of the controls in that setting or (2) an unwillingness to implement good controls. An imperfect understanding of the situation may be due to any of a number of things. One thing that many of the firms on this list have in common is that they are growing rapidly. Rapid growth often precipitates control problems because it causes the key factors that need to be controlled tightly to change; it may also cause management to delay the development of adequate controls, usually while marketing is emphasized.[39]

Personal style also makes some managers unwilling to implement a proper set of controls, at least on a timely basis. Entrepreneurs, particularly, often find it difficult to relinquish the centralized control they exerted when their firm was small in order to adopt a more appropriate set of controls. This may be the case at Warner Communications, as Warner's chairman, Steven Ross, "seems uninterested in building formal structures to protect Warner from repeating past mistakes."[40]

Criticisms, however, should be made very carefully. While many companies — probably including most of those mentioned in the list above — do have control system weaknesses of various magnitudes, knowing what should be criticized is not easy. Not all control systems that do not look as "neat" and "efficient" as they might be are deserving of criticism. It is not easy to keep a finely tuned set of controls in place, particularly when the company or function is operating in rapidly changing environments, and it may actually be desirable to implement control systems that are seemingly sloppy because these systems can minimize some of the harmful control system side effects. Digital Equipment Corporation has what could be described as a rather loose control system with, for example, unclear lines of authority, but Digital's management sees their company's "controlled chaos" as a virtue; and it has indeed probably contributed to the company's considerable success over the years.

The explication of the advantages of control systems that are not too tidy has been presented several times recently in the research literature. One of the major conclusions coming out of Richard Vancil's large empirical study was that allowing "ambiguity" in the roles of profit center managers in decentralized firms is natural and not necessarily undesirable.[41] And Bo Hedberg and Sten Jönsson suggest that "semi-confusing" information systems might be better than well-defined, well-established systems, especially in changing environments, because they can help keep the people in the organization alert for changes and receptive to them.[42]

So criticisms of control systems must be made with great caution. Controls that seem sloppy may have some unseen benefits, such as in terms of high creativity, a healthy spirit of cooperation, or low cost. Even the suffering of ill effects due to the occurrence of one or more of the control problems does not necessarily mean that a poor control system was in place: Control systems only reduce the probability of poor performance; they do not eliminate it.

The important point is that most criticisms should be leveled only after a thorough investigation of the situation. Control looms as a very complex part of the management function. There is no perfect control system; there is no one best way to accomplish good control; and there are many control benefits and costs that are not apparent at first glance.

CONCLUSION

This book has attempted to provide a new look at the subject of controls in organizations and a new way of conceptualizing some of the key control decisions managers have to make. Authors writing about control in organizations often focus very narrowly, perhaps only on one type of control, and they do not always make it clear that managers can use many devices as substitutes for each other. The intent here was to provide a broader focus.

The book began with a description of the problems that necessitate controls and control systems and a definition of the objective — good control. Considerable discussion unraveled a basic method of classifying the many available control tools according to the object of control. This classification is admittedly a first cut, but it is perhaps the cleanest, most meaningful categorization of controls, and it should provide a basic building block upon which more detailed classification schemes can be built. Finally, this classification scheme was related to some of the major control issues organizations face, particularly the choice of the object of control and the decision as to how tightly or loosely to apply the controls.

Some suggestions have been provided here, but more specific, more certain answers remain beyond reach with the current state of knowledge. In particular, we need to know more about the *behaviors* of individuals and groups in organizational settings and how they can be influenced.

NOTES

1. For general discussions of how goals and objectives can be stated and how the statements affect the messages they deliver, see Kenneth J. Euske, *Management Control: Planning, Control, Measurement, and Evaluation* (Reading, Mass.: Addison-Wesley, 1984); and Max D. Richards, *Organizational Goal Structures* (St. Paul, Minn.: West, 1978).
2. Peter F. Drucker, *Management: Tasks, Responsibilities, Practices* (New York: Harper & Row, 1974), p. 220.
3. David H. Maister, "Hewitt Associates," case no. 2–681–063 (Boston: HBS Case Services, 1981).
4. The original statement of this idea of a short list of critical success factors was probably in an article by D. Ronald Daniel ("Management Information Crisis," *Harvard Business Review* 39 [September-October 1961]: 120). In the years since that article was published, other authors have expressed the same idea but using a variety of terms, including *key success factors, key variables,* or *pulse points.*
5. John F. Rockart, "Chief Executives Define Their Own Data Needs," *Harvard Business Review* LVIII (March-April 1979): 85.
6. Robert N. Anthony and John Dearden, *Management Control Systems* (Homewood, Ill.: Richard D. Irwin, 1980), p. 89.
7. James Cook, "How to Beat the Recession — Any Recession," *Forbes,* December 20, 1982, p. 55.
8. Personal interview with the chairman of a small start-up company.
9. Richard F. Vancil, *Decentralization: Managerial Ambiguity by Design* (Homewood, Ill.: Dow Jones–Irwin, 1979).
10. Interview with a general manager in a large, diversified corporation.
11. "JWT's 'Irregularities' Top $30 Million," New York *Times,* March 31, 1982, p. D2.
12. "MIKO Corporation," case no. 9–181–068 (Boston: HBS Case Services, 1980).

13. Quotation from Regan Rockhill, a white-collar crime specialist with the accounting firm of Laventhol & Horwath, in "How to Prevent an Employee from Ripping Off the Firm," *Wall Street Journal*, May 5, 1982, p. 33.
14. Max Weber, *The Theory of Social and Economic Organization,* trans. A. M. Henderson and Talcott Parsons (New York: Free Press, 1947), p. 337.
15. Victor Thompson, *Modern Organization* (New York: Alfred A. Knopf, 1961), pp. 152–77.
16. William J. Abernathy, Kim B. Clark, and Allen M. Kantrow, *Industrial Renaissance: Producing a Competitive Future for America* (New York: Basic Books, 1983), p. 128.
17. For example, see Edward E. Lawler III and John G. Rhode, *Information and Control in Organizations* (Pacific Palisades, Calif.: Goodyear, 1976).
18. Thomas J. Peters and Robert H. Waterman, Jr., *In Search of Excellence* (New York: Harper & Row, 1982).
19. Ibid., p. 76.
20. Ibid., p. 105.
21. This observation has been made in a number of critiques of the Peters and Waterman book. See, for example, Daniel T. Carroll, "A Disappointing Search for Excellence," *Harvard Business Review* 83 (November-December 1983): 78–88; and Bro Uttal, "The Corporate Culture Vultures," *Fortune,* October 17, 1983, pp. 66–72.
22. Vijay Sathe, "Demystifying Corporate Culture" (Working Paper no. 83–22, Graduate School of Business Administration, Harvard University, 1983).
23. D. Daryl Wyckoff and W. Earl Sasser, *The Chain-Restaurant Industry* (Lexington, Mass.: Lexington Books [D. C. Heath], 1978), p. lxv.
24. This is one of the central points made in Larry E. Greiner, "Evolution and Revolution as Organizations Grow," *Harvard Business Review* 50 (July-August 1972): 37–46.
25. Francis Jones and Regina Herzlinger, "Massport," case no. 9–179–169 (Boston: HBS Case Services, 1979).
26. See, for example, "Moscow Tries to Light a Fire under Its Workers," *Business Week,* August 1, 1983, p. 44; and David Brand, "Soviet Boss Takes Aim at Lax Work Habits to Rouse the Economy," *Wall Street Journal,* January 31, 1982, p. 1.
27. Daniel Burstein, "China Gropes for Perfect Blend of Management Techniques," *International Management* (April 1983): 57–64.
28. For example, a recent study conducted in large U.S. corporations concluded that money did not have strong motivating effects for top-level managers. See Gordon Donaldson and Jay W. Lorsch, *Decision Making at the Top* (New York: Basic Books, 1983).
29. Pat Joynt, Toni Whitmont, and Brian Groth, "A Comparative Analysis of Australian Organizational Behavior" (Working Paper no. 81/15, Norwegian School of Management, Oslo, Norway, 1981), p. 3.
30. Geert H. Hofstede, *Culture's Consequences: International Differences in Work-Related Values* (Beverly Hills, Calif.: Sage, 1980).
31. See, for example, Special Task Force to the Secretary of Health, Education and Welfare, *Work in America* (Cambridge, Mass.: Massachusetts Institute of Technology Press, 1973); and Jon E. Walker and Curt Tausky, "An Analysis of Work Incentives," *Journal of Social Psychology* 116 (1982): 27–39.

32. "How Steve Ross's Hands-Off Approach Is Backfiring at Warner," *Business Week*, August 8, 1983, pp. 70–71.
33. Kathleen K. Wiegner, "The One That Almost Got Away," *Forbes*, January 31, 1983, pp. 46–47.
34. Daron P. Levin, "Poor Controls at Rockwell Helped Make It a Fraud Victim, Report Says," *Wall Street Journal*, August 18, 1983, p. 25.
35. Stephen J. Sansweet, "Troubles at Mattel Seen Extending Beyond Fallout in Electronics Line," *Wall Street Journal*, December 1, 1983.
36. Heywood Klein, "Fast-Growing Company's Fall Attributed to Flawed Accounting and Risky Buyouts," *Wall Street Journal*, August 2, 1983, p. 31.
37. "Is the Worst Over for Fairchild Camera?" *Business Week*, November 14, 1983, p. 78.
38. Heywood Klein, "Zooming Firms of 1980 Find That Fast Growth Can Turn into a Curse," *Wall Street Journal*, August 24, 1983, p. 1.
39. Ibid.
40. "How Steve Ross's Hands-Off Approach Is Backfiring at Warner," p. 70.
41. Vancil, *Decentralization*.
42. Bo Hedberg and Sten Jönsson, "Designing Semi-Confusing Information Systems for Organizations in Changing Environments," *Accounting, Organizations and Society* 3 (1978): 47–64.

BIBLIOGRAPHY

Abernathy, William J., Kim B. Clark, and Allen M. Kantrow. *Industrial Renaissance: Producing a Competitive Future for America*. New York: Basic Books, 1983.

"An Acid Test for Tandem's Growth." *Business Week,* February 28, 1983, p. 64.

Albrecht, W. Steve, and Marshall B. Romney. "Deterring White-Collar Crime in Banks." *Banker's Magazine* 163 (November–December 1980): 60–64.

Alderman, C. Wayne, Glenn E. Summers, and Mary Jeanne Welsh. "The Trend toward Soft Data in Accounting." *Management Accounting* LXV (December 1983): 34–39.

"American Bakeries: A New Chef Cleans Up the Kitchen." *Business Week,* June 27, 1983, p. 52.

American Institute of Certified Public Accountants, Operational Audit Engagements. (New York: American Institute of Certified Public Accountants, 1982).

Anthony, Robert N. "Cost Concepts for Control." *Accounting Review* 32 (April 1957): 229–30.

———. *Planning and Control Systems: A Framework for Analysis*. Boston, Mass.: Division of Research, Graduate School of Business Administration, Harvard University, 1965.

Anthony, Robert N., and John Dearden. *Management Control Systems*. Homewood, Ill.: Richard D. Irwin, 1980.

Argyris, Chris. *The Impact of Budgets on People*. Ithaca, N.Y.: School of Business and Public Administration, Cornell University, 1952.

———. *Personality and Organization*. New York: Harper & Row, 1957.

Arrow, Kenneth J. "Control in Large Organizations." In *Behavioral Aspects of Accounting,* edited by Michael Schiff and Arie Y. Lewin, pp. 275–84. Englewood Cliffs, N.J.: Prentice-Hall, 1974.

———. *The Limits of Organization*. New York: W. W. Norton, 1974.

Arvey, Richard D. *Fairness in Selecting Employees*. Reading, Mass.: Addison-Wesley, 1979.

"As Many of the Big Eight Centralize, Price Waterhouse Bucks the Trend." *Business Week,* October 24, 1983, pp. 114–18.

Ashton, Robert H. *Human Information Processing in Accounting.* no. 17. Studies in Accounting Research. Sarasota, Fla.: American Accounting Association, 1982.

"Atari's Struggle to Stay Ahead." *Business Week,* September 13, 1982, p. 56.

"Automaking on a Human Scale." *Fortune,* April 5, 1982, pp. 89–93.

Babchuk, N., and W. J. Goode. "Work Incentives in a Self-Determined Group." *American Social Review* 16 (1951): 679–87.

Bales, Carter F. "Strategic Control: The President's Paradox." *Business Horizons* 20 (August 1977): 17–28.

Ball, Robert. "A 'Shopkeeper' Shakes Up Nestlé." *Fortune,* December 27, 1982, pp. 103–6.

Banker, Rajiv D., and Joseph G. San Miguel. "Portland General Electric Company." case no. 9–178–171. (Boston: HBS Case Services, 1978).

Banks, H. "People Power." *Forbes,* April 25, 1983, p. 170.

Beaver, William H. *Financial Reporting: An Accounting Revolution.* Englewood Cliffs, N.J.: Prentice-Hall, 1981.

Beaver, William H., and Wayne R. Landsman. *Incremental Information Content of Statement 33 Disclosures.* (Stamford, Conn.: Financial Accounting Standards Board, 1983).

Beaver, William H., Paul A. Griffin, and Wayne R. Landsman. "The Incremental Information Content of Replacement Cost Earnings." *Journal of Accounting and Economics* 4 (1982): 15–39.

"Behind the UPS Mystique: Puritanism and Productivity." *Business Week,* June 6, 1983, p. 66.

"Big Business Tries to Imitate the Entrepreneurial Spirit." *Business Week,* April 18, 1983, pp. 84–89.

Blau, Peter M. *The Dynamics of Bureaucracy.* Chicago: University of Chicago Press, 1955.

Bodie, Zvi. " 'Compound-Interest' Depreciation in Capital Investment." *Harvard Business Review* 60 (May–June 1982): 58–60.

Bower, Joseph L. "Solving the Problems of Business Policy." *Journal of Business Strategy* 2 (Winter 1982): 32–44.

Brand, David. "Soviet Boss Takes Aim at Lax Work Habits to Rouse the Economy." *Wall Street Journal,* January 31, 1982, p. 1.

Brehm, Jack W., and Arthur R. Cohen. *Explorations in Cognitive Dissonance.* New York: John Wiley, 1958.

Brief, Richard P. "The Origin and Evolution of Nineteenth-Century Asset Accounting." *Business History Review* XL (1966): 1–2.

Briloff, Abraham J. *Unaccountable Accounting.* New York: Harper & Row, 1972.

Brindisi, Louis J. "Executive Compensation Programs Go Wrong." *Wall Street Journal,* June 14, 1982, p. 20.

Brownell, Peter. "Participation in the Budgeting Process — When It Works and When It Doesn't." *Journal of Accounting Literature* 1 (Spring 1982): 124–53.

Brumback, Gary B. "Revisiting an Approach to Managing Behaviors and Results." *Public Personnel Management Journal* 10 (Summer 1981): 270–77.

Bruns, William J., Jr., and John H. Waterhouse. "Budgetary Control and Organization Structure." *Journal of Accounting Research* 13 (Autumn 1975): 177–203.

Burstein, Daniel. "China Gropes for Perfect Blend of Management Techniques." *International Management* 38 (April 1983): 57–64.

Cammann, Cortlandt. "Effects of the Use of Control Systems." *Accounting, Organizations and Society* 1 (1976): 301–14.

"Capital Offense." *Forbes,* January 17, 1983, pp. 100–101.

Carroll, Daniel T. "A Disappointing Search for Excellence." *Harvard Business Review* 83 (November–December 1983): 78–88.

Chace, Susan, and Michael W. Miller. "Commodore's Tramiel Sharpens Competition in Small Computers." *Wall Street Journal,* August 18, 1983, p. 1.

Chatfield, Michael. *A History of Accounting Thought.* Hinsdale, Ill.: Dryden Press, 1974.

Child, John. "Strategies of Control and Organizational Behavior." *Administrative Science Quarterly* 18 (March 1973): 1–17.

"Chip Wars: The Japanese Threat." *Business Week,* May 23, 1983, p. 80.

Clark, Rodney. *The Japanese Company.* New Haven, CT: The Yale University Press, 1979.

Cloninger, Dale O. "American Myopia." *Collegiate Forum* (Fall 1981): 6.

Collins, Frank. "The Interaction of Budget Characteristics and Personality Variables with Budgetary Response Attitudes." *Accounting Review* LIII (April 1978): 324–35.

"Conglomerate Managers Fall into Step, too." *Business Week,* February 6, 1984, p. 50.

"The Controller: Inflation Gives Him More Clout with Management." *Business Week,* August 15, 1977, p. 84.

Cook, James. "How to Beat the Recession — Any Recession." *Forbes,* December 20, 1982, p. 50.

"Cooking the Books." *Dun's Business Month* 120 (January 1983): 40.

Curtis, Carol E. "Texaco's Single-Minded Boss." *Business Week,* May 9, 1983, p. 61.

Cyert, Richard M., and James G. March. *A Behavioral Theory of the Firm.* Englewood Cliffs, N.J.: Prentice-Hall, 1963.

Dalton, Gene W. "Motivation and Control in Organizations." In *Motivation and Control in Organizations,* edited by Gene W. Dalton and Paul R. Lawrence, pp. 1–35. Homewood, Ill.: Richard D. Irwin and the Dorsey Press, 1971.

Daniel, Donald R. "Management Information Crisis." *Harvard Business Review* 39 (September–October 1961): 111–21.

"Data General's Management Trouble." *Business Week,* February 9, 1981, p. 58.

Dearden, John. "The Case against ROI Control." *Harvard Business Review* XLVII (May–June 1969): 124–35.

Dermer, Jerry. *Management Planning and Control Systems.* Homewood, Ill.: Richard D. Irwin, 1977.

"Did Warner-Lambert Make a $468 Million Mistake?" *Business Week,* November 21, 1983, p. 123.

Donaldson, Gordon, and Jay W. Lorsch. *Decision Making at the Top.* New York: Basic Books, 1983.

Dougherty, Philip H. "JWT's 'Irregularities' Top $30 Million." *New York Times,* March 31, 1982, pp. D1–D2.

Drucker, Peter F. "Controls, Control and Management." In *Management Controls: New*

Directions in Basic Research, edited by Charles P. Bonini, Robert K. Jaedicke, and Harvey M. Wagner, pp. 286–96. New York: McGraw-Hill, 1964.

———. *Management: Tasks, Responsibilities, Practices.* New York: Harper & Row, 1974.

Edström, Anders, and Jay R. Galbraith. "Transfer of Managers as a Coordination and Control Strategy in Multinational Organizations." *Administrative Science Quarterly* 22 (June 1977): 248–63.

"Emerson Electric: High Profits from Low Tech." *Business Week,* April 4, 1983, p. 58.

"Europe's New Managers: Going Global with a U.S. Style." *Business Week,* May 24, 1982, p. 116.

Euske, Kenneth J. *Management Control: Planning, Control, Measurement, and Evaluation.* Reading, Mass.: Addison–Wesley, 1984.

"Executive Compensation: Looking to the Long Term Again." *Business Week,* May 9, 1983, pp. 80–83.

"Executives Keep Reducing the Risks of a High-Reward Career." *Business Week,* May 9, 1983, p. 83.

Fabozzi, Frank J., and Robert Fonfeder. "Have You Seen Any Good Quarterly Statements Lately?" *Journal of Portfolio Management* 9 (Winter 1983): 71–74.

Fast, Norman, and Norman A. Berg. "The Lincoln Electric Company." case no. 9–376–028. (Boston: HBS Case Services, 1975).

Faux, Victor. "Unobtrusive Controls in Organizations: An Action Research Approach to Organizational Change." Ph.D. diss., Harvard University, 1981.

Fialka, John J. "Ailing Computers Give Social Security System Another Big Problem." *Wall Street Journal,* October 5. 1981, p. 1.

Financial Accounting Standards Board. *Accounting for Research and Development Costs: Statement of Financial Accounting Standards no. 2.* (Stamford, Conn.: Financial Accounting Standards Board, 1974).

———. *Financial Reporting and Changing Prices: Statement of Accounting Standards no. 33.* (Stamford, Conn.: Financial Accounting Standards Board, 1979).

———. *Qualitative Characteristics of Accounting Information: Statement of Financial Accounting Concepts no. 2.* (Stamford, Conn.: Financial Accounting Standards Board, 1980).

Fischhoff, Baruch. "Hindsight/Foresight: The Effect of Outcome Knowledge on Judgment under Uncertainty." *Journal of Experimental Psychology: Human Perception and Performance* 1 (May 1975): 288–99.

Fischhoff, Baruch, and Ruth Beyth. " 'I Knew It Would Happen' — Remembered Probabilities of Once-Future Things." *Organizational Behavior and Human Performance* 13 (February 1975): 1–16.

Flamholtz, Eric G. "Behavioral Aspects of Accounting/Control Systems." In *Organizational Behavior,* edited by Steven Kerr, pp. 289–316. Columbus, Ohio: Grid, 1979.

———. *Human Resource Accounting.* Encino, Calif.: Dickinson, 1974.

———. "Organizational Control Systems as a Managerial Tool." *California Management Review* XXII (Winter 1979): 50–59.

Ford, Charles H. "Manage by Decisions, Not by Objectives." *Business Horizons* 23 (February 1980): 7–18.

————. "MBO: An Idea Whose Time Has Gone." *Business Horizons* 22 (December 1979): 54.

Freeman, Alan, and John Urquart. "Hard-Working Irvings Maintain Tight Control in a Canadian Province." *Wall Street Journal,* November 1, 1983, p. 1.

Galbraith, Jay R. *Organization Design.* Reading, Mass.: Addison-Wesley, 1977.

Getschow, George. "Slick Accounting Ploys Help Many Companies Improve Their Income." *Wall Street Journal,* June 20, 1980, p. 1.

Gillmor, Dan. "Crime Is Headed Up — And So Is Business." *Boston Globe,* February 15, 1983, p. 35.

"Gould Loosens Up as It Gains in High-Tech, But Some Doubt Strong Chief Will Let Go." *Wall Street Journal,* May 26, 1983, p. 33.

Govindarajan, Vijayaraghavan, and Joseph G. San Miguel. "Sears, Roebuck and Co. (C): The Internal Audit Function." case no. 9–179–125. (Boston: HBS Case Services, 1979).

Grant, John L. "Inflation's Full Impact on the Bottom Line." *Business Week,* February 7, 1983, p. 8.

Greiner, Larry E. "Evolution and Revolution as Organizations Grow." *Harvard Business Review* 50 (July-August 1972): 37–46.

Guyon, Janet. "The Public Doesn't Get a Better Potato Chip without a Bit of Pain." *Wall Street Journal,* March 25, 1983, p. 1.

Harris, Roy J., Jr. "New Airline Surmounting Labor Dilemma." *Wall Street Journal,* September 12, 1983, p. 35.

Hayden, Trudy. "Employers Who Use Lie Detector Tests." *Business and Society Review* 41 (Spring 1982): 16–21.

Hayes, Robert H., and William J. Abernathy. "Managing Our Way to Economic Decline." *Harvard Business Review* 58 (July-August 1980): 67–77.

Hedberg, Bo, and Sten Jönsson. "Designing Semi-Confusing Information Systems for Organizations in Changing Environments." *Accounting, Organizations and Society* 3 (1978): 47–64.

Heider, Fritz. "Attitudes and Cognitive Organization." *Journal of Psychology* 21 (January 1946): 107–12.

Helyar, John. "Big Continental Illinois Hopes It Will Recover as U.S. Economy Does." *Wall Street Journal,* January 5, 1983, p. 1.

"The Hennessy Style May Be What Allied Needs." *Business Week,* Januiary 11, 1982, p. 126.

Henrici, Stanley. "The Perversity, Peril and Pathos of ROI." *Financial Analysts Journal* 39 (September-October 1983): 79–80.

Herzlinger, Regina. "The Hyatt Hill Health Center." case no. 9–172–309. (Boston: HBS Case Services, 1972).

Herzlinger, Regina, and Frederic Hooper. "The Impact of Financial Information: An Empirical Study of Professionals in a Nonprofit Organization." Working Paper, Graduate School of Business Administration, Harvard University, March 1983.

Hirschman, Albert O. *Exit, Voice and Loyalty: Responses to Decline in Firms, Organizations and States.* Cambridge, Mass.: Harvard University Press, 1970.

Hofstede, Geert H. *Culture's Consequences: International Differences in Work-Related Values*. Beverly Hills, Calif.: Sage, 1980.

———. *The Game of Budget Control*. Assen, The Netherlands: Van Gorcum, 1967.

———. "Management Control of Public and Not-for-Profit Activities." *Accounting, Organizations and Society* 6 (1981): 193–216.

Hollinger, Richard C., and John P. Clark. *Theft by Employees*. Lexington, Mass.: Lexington Books, 1983.

Holt, Robert N., and Rebecca E. Fincher. "The Foreign Corrupt Practices Act." *Financial Analysts Journal* 37 (March–April 1981): 73–76.

"Honeywell's Survival Plan in Computers." *Business Week,* May 23, 1983, p. 108.

Hooper, Paul, and John Page. "Internal Control Problems in Computer Systems." *Journal of Systems Management* 33 (December 1982): 22–27.

Hopwood, Anthony G. *Accounting and Human Behaviour*. Englewood Cliffs, N.J.: Prentice-Hall, 1976.

Horngren, Charles T. *Cost Accounting: A Managerial Emphasis*. Englewood Cliffs, N.J.: Prentice-Hall, 1982.

———. "Inflation and Internal Accounting." In *Current Cost Accounting, Its Aspects and Impacts: Proceedings of April 1983 Conference,* edited by Adolph J.H. Enthoven, chapter 9. (Dallas: Center for International Accounting Development, University of Texas at Dallas, 1983).

Horwitz, Bertrand N., and Richard Kolodny. "The Economic Effects of Involuntary Uniformity in the Financial Reporting of R & D Expenditures." *Journal of Accounting Research* (supp. 1980): 38–74.

"How a Winning Formula Can Fail." *Business Week,* May 25, 1981, pp. 119–20.

"How Signode's Managers Turned into Entrepreneurs." *Business Week,* June 6, 1983, p. 86.

"How Steve Ross's Hands-Off Approach Is Backfiring at Warner." *Business Week,* August 8, 1983, pp. 70–71.

"How to Manage Entrepreneurs." *Business Week,* September 7, 1981, p. 69.

"How to Prevent an Employee from Ripping Off the Firm." *Wall Street Journal,* May 5, 1982, p. 33.

Hudson, Richard L. "SEC Charges Fudging of Corporate Figures Is a Growing Practice." *Wall Street Journal,* June 2, 1983, p. 1.

Huey, John. "New Top Executives Shake Up Old Order at Soft-Drink Giant." *Wall Street Journal,* November 6, 1981, p. 1.

Ijiri, Yuji. "On the Accountability-Based Framework of Accounting." *Journal of Accounting and Public Policy* 2 (Summer 1983): 75–82.

"Is the Worst Over for Fairchild Camera?" *Business Week,* November 14, 1983, p. 78.

"ITT: Groping for a New Strategy." *Business Week,* December 15, 1980, pp. 66–80.

Jacobs, Sanford L. "Experts Say Computerization Raises Risk of Embezzlement." *Wall Street Journal,* February 28, 1981, p. 25.

"Jerry Reinsdorf Pulls a Double Play in Chicago." *Business Week,* October 10, 1983, p. 53.

Johnson, Jan. "Comserv Does Its Books." *Datamation* 29 (December 1983): 55–66.

Jones, Francis, and Regina Herzlinger. "Massport." case no. 9–179–169. (Boston: HBS Case Services, 1979).

Joynt, Pat, Toni Whitmont, and Brian Groth. "A Comparative Analysis of Australian Organizational Behavior." Working Paper no. 81/15, Norwegian School of Management, Oslo, Norway, 1981.

Kamin, Jacob Y., and Joshua Ronen. "Effects of Budgetary Control Design on Management Decisions: Some Empirical Evidence." *Decision Sciences* 12 (July 1981): 471–85.

Kaplan, Robert S. *Advanced Management Accounting.* Englewood Cliffs, N.J.: Prentice-Hall, 1981.

———. "Measuring Manufacturing Performance: A New Challenge for Managerial Accounting Research." *Accounting Review* LVIII (October 1983): 686–705.

Katz, Daniel, and Robert L. Kahn. *The Social Psychology of Organizations.* 2d ed. New York: Wiley, 1978.

Kell, Walter G., and Richard E. Ziegler. *Modern Auditing.* Boston: Warren, Gorham & Lamont, 1980.

Keller, Robert T., and Andrew D. Szilagyi. "Employee Reactions to Leader Reward Behavior." *Academy of Management Journal* 19 (December 1976): 619–27.

Kerr, Steven. "On the Folly of Rewarding A While Hoping for B." *Academy of Management Journal* 18 (December 1975): 769–83.

Ketz, J. Edward. "Are Constant Dollar Disclosures Informative?" *Financial Analysts Journal* 39 (March-April 1983): 52–55.

Klein, Heywood. "At Harley-Davidson, Life without AMF Is Upbeat But Full of Financial Problems." *Wall Street Journal,* April 13, 1982, p. 37.

———. "Fast-Growing Company's Fall Attributed to Flawed Accounting and Risky Buyouts." *Wall Street Journal,* August 2, 1983, p. 31.

———. "Gould Loosens Up as It Gains in High-Tech, But Some Doubt Strong Chief Will Let Go." *Wall Street Journal,* May 26, 1983, p. 33.

———. "Zooming Firms of 1980 Find That Fast Growth Can Turn into a Curse." *Wall Street Journal,* August 24, 1983, p. 1.

Koeneke, W. "Forms Control — Fortune or Flop?" *Journal of Systems Management* 32 (January 1981): 11–14.

Kotter, John P., Leonard A. Schlesinger, and Vijay Sathe. *Organization: Text, Cases, and Readings on the Management of Organizational Design and Change.* Homewood, Ill.: Richard D. Irwin, 1979.

Lancaster, Hal, and G. Christian Hill. "Fraud at Wells Fargo Depended on Avoiding Computer's Red Flags." *Wall Street Journal,* February 26, 1981, p. 1.

Landau, Martin, and Russell Stout, Jr. "To Manage Is Not to Control: Or the Folly of Type II Errors." *Public Administration Review* 39 (March-April 1979): 148–56.

Landro, Laura. "Analysis of ITT's Report Shows Problems in Halting Questionable Foreign Payments." *Wall Street Journal,* June 3, 1982, p. 27.

Larcker, David F. "The Association between Performance Plan Adoption and Corporate Capital Investment." *Journal of Accounting and Economics* 5 (1983): 3–30.

Larson, Erik, and Carrie Dolan. "Once All Alone in Field, Apple Computer Girds for Industry Shakeout." *Wall Street Journal,* October 4, 1983, p. 1.

Larson, Erik, and Ken Wells. "Shaken Osborne Computer Seeking Suitor in the Face of Possible Failure." *Wall Street Journal,* September 12, 1983, p. 35.

Lawler, Edward E. III. "Control Systems in Organizations." In *Handbook of Industrial and Organizational Psychology,* edited by Marvin Dunnette, pp. 1247–91. Skokie, Ill.: Rand McNally, 1975.

———. *Pay and Organization Development.* Reading, Mass.: Addison-Wesley, 1980.

Lawler, Edward E. III, and John G. Rhode. *Information and Control in Organizations.* Pacific Palisades, Calif.: Goodyear, 1976.

Lee, Robert G. "How H. Ross Perot Builds Fierce Loyalty at EDS in Dallas." *International Management* 38 (March 1983): 33.

"Letter to Shareholders." Xerox Corporation, 1982 Annual Report.

Levin, Doron P. "Poor Controls at Rockwell Helped Make It a Fraud Victim, Report Says." *Wall Street Journal,* August 18, 1983, p. 25.

Libby, Robert. *Accounting and Human Information Processing: Theory and Applications.* Englewood Cliffs, N.J.: Prentice-Hall, 1981.

Lipman, Mark. *Stealing: How America's Employees Are Stealing Their Companies Blind.* New York: Harper's Magazine Press, 1973.

"Listening to the Voice of the Marketplace." *Business Week,* February 21, 1983, p. 90.

Locke, Edwin A., Karyll N. Shaw, Lise M. Saari, and Gary Latham. "Goal Setting and Task Performance: 1969–1980." *Psychological Bulletin* 90 (1981): 125–52.

Loomis, Carol J. "How GE Manages Inflation." *Fortune,* May 4, 1981, pp. 121–24.

——— "The Madness of Executive Compensation." *Fortune,* July 12, 1982, pp. 42–52.

Lorange, Peter. "Strategic Control: Some Issues in Making It Operationally More Useful." Paper presented at the First European Conference on Corporate Planning, Fontainebleau, France, June 24, 1980.

McCaskey, Michael B. *The Executive Challenge: Managing Change and Ambiguity.* Marshfield, Mass.: Pitman Publishing Inc., 1982.

McGowan, William. "The Great White-Collar Crime Coverup." *Business and Society Review* 45 (Spring 1983): 25–31.

McGregor, Douglas. *The Professional Manager.* New York: McGraw-Hill, 1967.

Maister, David H. "Hewitt Associates." case no. 2–681–063. (Boston: HBS Case Services, 1981).

March, James G., and Herbert A. Simon. *Organizations.* New York: Wiley, 1958.

Merchant, Kenneth A. "Analog Devices, Inc. (A)." case no. 9–181–001. (Boston: HBS Case Services, 1980).

———. "The Control Function of Management." *Sloan Management Review* 23 (Summer 1982): 43–55.

———. "Control in Organizations: A Literature Review." Working Paper no. 83–69, Graduate School of Business Administration, Harvard University, 1983.

———. "ES, Inc." case no. 9–183–061. (Boston: HBS Case Services, 1982).

———. "The Effects of Organizational Controls." Working Paper, Graduate School of Business Administration, Harvard University, 1984.

Merchant, Kenneth A., and Thomas V. Bonoma. "Macon Prestressed Concrete Company (A)-(D)." case nos. 9–182–175, 9–182–176, 9–182–177, 9–182–266. (Boston: HBS Case Services, 1982).

Merchant, Kenneth A., and William J. Bruns, Jr. "Measure Better, Manage Better: A Cure for Management Myopia." Working Paper no. 83–83, Graduate School of Business Administration, Harvard University, 1983.

Mesdag, Lisa Miller. "The 50 Largest Private Industrial Companies." *Fortune,* May 31, 1982, p. 108.

Meyer, H. H. "The Pay-for-Performance Dilemma." *Organizational Dynamics* 4 (Winter 1975): 39–50.

"MIKO Corporation." case no. 9–181–068. (Boston: HBS Case Services, 1980).

Mitchell, David. *Control without Bureaucracy.* London: McGraw-Hill, 1979.

Betsy Morris. "Accounting Scams Are on the Rise, Putting More Pressure on Auditors." *Wall Street Journal,* July 9, 1982, p. 19.

––––––. "After a Long Simmer, The Pot Boils Again at Campbell Soup Co." *Wall Street Journal,* July 16, 1982, p. 1.

––––––. "McCormick & Co. Division Is Found to Use Dubious Accounting Methods to Boost Net." *Wall Street Journal,* June 1, 1982, p. 10.

"Moscow Tries to Light a Fire under Its Workers." *Business Week,* August 1, 1983, p. 44.

Mrowca, Maryann. "Ohio Firm Relies on Incentive-Pay System to Motivate Workers and Maintain Products." *Wall Street Journal,* August 12, 1983, p. 23.

Mruk, Edwin S., and James A. Giardina. "Executive Compensation: Tenth Edition Study." *Financial Executive* L (October 1982): 42–50.

––––––. "Executive Compensation: Eleventh Edition Study." *Financial Executive* LI (October 1983): 42–50.

Mufson, Steve. "Amerada Hess Chief Keeps Controls Tight, Emphasizes Marketing." *Wall Street Journal,* January 11, 1983, p. 1.

"The New Entrepreneurs." *Business Week,* April 18, 1983, p. 78.

Nisbett, Richard E., and Lee Ross. *Human Inference: Strategies and Shortcomings of Social Judgment.* Englewood Cliffs, N.J.: Prentice-Hall, 1980.

Norris, William C. "How to Expand R & D Cooperation." *Business Week,* April 11, 1983, p. 21.

Odiorne, George. *Management by Objectives: A System of Management Leadership.* Belmont, Calif.: Pitman Learning Inc. 1965.

Onsi, Mohamed. "Factor Analysis of Behavioral Variables Affecting Budgetary Slack." *Accounting Review* XLVIII (October 1973): 535–48.

"Operation Turnaround." *Business Week,* December 5, 1983, p. 124.

Otley, David T. "Budget Use and Managerial Performance." *Journal of Accounting Research* 16 (Spring 1978): 122–49.

Otley, David T., and A. J. Berry. "Control, Organization and Accounting." *Accounting, Organizations and Society* 5 (1980): 231–46.

Ouchi, William G. "A Conceptual Framework for the Design of Organizational Control Mechanisms." *Management Science* 25 (September 1979): 833–48.

––––––. *Theory Z: How American Business Can Meet the Japanese Challenge.* Reading, Mass.: Addison-Wesley, 1981.

Ouchi, William G., and Alfred M. Jaeger. "Type Z Organization: Stability in the Midst of Mobility." *Academy of Management Review* 3 (April 1978): 305–14.

Pascale, Richard T., and Anthony G. Athos. *The Art of Japanese Management.* New York: Simon & Schuster, 1981.

Peters, Thomas J. "Putting Excellence into Management." *Business Week,* July 21, 1980, p. 196.

Peters, Thomas J., and Robert H. Waterman, Jr. *In Search of Excellence*. New York: Harper & Row, 1982.

Prakash, Prem, and Alfred Rappaport. "Informational Interdependencies: System Structure Induced by Accounting Information." *Accounting Review* L (October 1975): 723–34.

"Prime Computer Sees Net Down in 2nd Period But Up for Full Year." *Wall Street Journal,* May 18, 1983, p. 20.

Pugh, Derek S., David J. Hickson, C. R. Hinings, and C. Turner. "Dimensions of Organization Structure." *Administrative Science Quarterly* 13 (1968): 65–105.

Raia, Anthony P. "Goal Setting and Self-Control: An Empirical Study." *Journal of Management Studies* 2 (February 1965): 34–53.

Rappaport, Alfred. "Corporate Performance Standards and Shareholder Value." *Journal of Business Strategy* 3 (Spring 1983): 28–38.

———. "Selecting Strategies That Create Shareholder Value." *Harvard Business Review* 59 (May–June 1981): 139–49.

Reece, James S., and William R. Cool. "Measuring Investment Center Performance." *Harvard Business Review* 56 (May–June 1978): 28–49.

Rhode, John G., and Fulton M. Smith, Jr. "Cost Accounting and Organizational Behavior." In *The Managerial and Cost Accountant's Handbook,* edited by Homer A. Black and James D. Edwards, pp. 257–94. Homewood, Ill.: Dow Jones–Irwin, 1979.

Richards, Max D. *Organizational Goal Structures*. St. Paul, Minn.: West Publishing Co., 1978.

Ridgway, V. F. "Dysfunctional Consequences of Performance Measurements." In *Information for Decision Making,* edited by Alfred Rappaport, pp. 378–83. Englewood Cliffs, N.J.: Prentice-Hall, 1982.

Ritchie, J. B., and Raymond E. Miles. "An Analysis of Quantity and Quality of Participation as Mediating Variables in the Participative Decision-Making Process." *Personnel Psychology* 23 (1970): 347–59.

Rockart, John F. "Chief Executives Define Their Own Data Needs." *Harvard Business Review* LVII (March–April 1979): 81–93.

Rohmann, Laura. "Write You Are." *Forbes,* May 9, 1983, p. 185.

Roush, Charles H., Jr., and Ben C. Ball, Jr. "Controlling the Implementation of Strategy." *Managerial Planning* 29 (November–December 1980): 3–12.

Sahlman, William A., and M. Edgar Barrett. "Laitier, S. A." case no. 9–176–118. (Boston: HBS Case Services, 1975).

Salamon, Julie. "How New York Bank Got Itself Entangled in Drysdale's Dealings." *Wall Street Journal,* June 11, 1982, p. 1.

Sansweet, Stephen J. "Troubles at Mattel Seen Extending Beyond Fallout in Electronics Line." *Wall Street Journal,* December 1, 1983, p. 31.

Sathe, Vijay. "Demystifying Corporate Culture." Working Paper no. 83–22, Graduate School of Business Administration, Harvard University, 1983.

Sayles, Leonard. "The Many Dimensions of Control." *Organizational Dynamics* 1 (Summer 1972): 21–31.

Schein, Edgar. "The Role of the Founder in the Creation of Organizational Culture."

Working Paper no. 1407–83, Alfred P. Sloan School of Management, Massachusetts Institute of Technology, 1983.

Schiff, Michael, and Arie Y. Lewin. "Where Traditional Budgeting Fails." *Financial Executive* 36 (May 1968): 50–62.

Schlender, Brenton R. "Datapoint Kept Trying to Set Profit Records Until the Bubble Burst." *Wall Street Journal,* May 27, 1982, p. 1.

Schmidt, R. R. "Executive Dishonesty: Misuse of Authority for Personal Gain." In *Internal Theft: Investigation and Control,* edited by Sheryl Leininger, pp. 69–81. Los Angeles: Security World, 1975.

"SEC Halts Spread of Accounting Method That Increases Profit of Software Firms." *Wall Street Journal,* April 15, 1983, p. 10.

Securities and Exchange Commission. "Adoption of Requirements for Financial Accounting and Reporting Practices for Oil and Gas Producing Activities." Accounting Series Release no. 253, August 31, 1978.

———. "Oil and the Producers — Supplemental Disclosures on the Basis of Reserve Recognition Accounting." Accounting Series Release no. 269, September 24, 1979.

Seed, Allen H. III. "New Approaches to Asset Management." *Journal of Business Strategy* 3 (Winter 1983): 16–22.

Selznick, Philip. *Leadership in Administration: A Sociological Interpretation.* New York: Row, Peterson, 1957.

Shaffer, Richard A. "Simulating Human Thought in Computers Proving Elusive." *Wall Street Journal,* August 5, 1983, p. 23.

Shillinglaw, Gordon. *Managerial Cost Accounting.* Homewood, Ill.: Richard D. Irwin, 1982.

"The Shrinking of Middle Management." *Business Week,* April 25, 1983, p. 55.

Simons, Robert L. "Control in Organizations: A Framework for Analysis." *Proceedings of the Canadian Academic Accounting Association Annual Conference,* 1982, pp. 101–113.

"Singapore Slings — and Arrows." *Economist,* October 2, 1982, p. 90.

Sloan, Alfred P., Jr. *My Years with General Motors.* New York: Doubleday, 1964.

Sloan, Allan. "Go Forth and Compete." *Forbes,* November 23, 1981, pp. 41–42.

Smith, Adam. *An Inquiry into the Nature and Causes of the Wealth of Nations.* 1776; reprinted ed., New York: Modern Library (Random House), 1937.

Smith, Geoffrey. "Hard Choices, the Hard Way." *Forbes,* November 7, 1983, p. 108.

Solomon, Ezra, and J. C. Laya. "Measurement of Company Profitability: Some Systematic Errors in the Accounting Rate of Return." In *Financial Research and Management Decisions,* edited by Alexander A. Robickek, pp. 152–79. New York: Wiley, 1967.

Solomons, David. *Divisional Performance: Measurement and Control.* Homewood, Ill.: Richard D. Irwin, 1965.

Special Task Force to the Secretary of Health, Education and Welfare. *Work in America.* Cambridge, Mass.: Massachusetts Institute of Technology Press, 1973.

"Spectra-Physics Sees Fiscal '83 Loss, Cites a $10 Million Charge." *Wall Street Journal,* August 9, 1983, p. 18.

Staubus, George J. *Making Accounting Decisions.* Houston: Scholars, 1977.

Stipp, David. "Texas Instruments Seeks Comeback Trail in Consumer Electronics; Outlook Is Hazy." *Wall Street Journal,* September 12, 1983, p. 4.

Stout, Russell, Jr. *Management or Control?: The Organizational Challenge.* Bloomington: Indiana University Press, 1980.

"A Takeover Hasn't Cramped Oppenheimer's Freewheeling Style." *Business Week,* October 10, 1983, p. 94.

"This Is the Answer." *Business Week,* July 5, 1982, pp. 50–52.

Thompson, Victor. *Modern Organization.* New York: Alfred A. Knopf, 1961.

Thurow, Lester C. "Where Management Fails." *Newsweek,* December 7, 1981, p. 78.

"Time Stealing." *Forbes,* December 20, 1982, p. 9.

Todd, Kenneth R., Jr. "How One Financial Officer Uses Inflation-Adjusted Accounting Data." *Financial Executive* 50 (October 1982): 13–19.

Tompor, Susan. "More Employers Attempt to Catch a Thief by Giving Job Applicants 'Honesty' Exams." *Wall Street Journal,* August 3, 1981, p. 17.

Traynor, Jeffrey M., and Kenneth A. Merchant. "Natomas North America (C)." case no. 9–184–033. (Boston: HBS Case Services, 1983).

Treynor, Jack L. "The Financial Objective in the Widely Held Corporation." *Financial Analysts Journal* 37 (March-April 1981): 68–71.

"TRW Leads a Revolution in Managing Technology." *Business Week,* November 15, 1982, p. 124.

"Turnover at the Top." *Business Week,* December 19, 1983, p. 104.

Ubelhart, Mark C. "A New Look at Executive Compensation Plans." *Cashflow* 2 (May 1981): 20–24.

Ulman, Neil. "Brazilian Oil Company Has Much of the Clout of Government Itself." *Wall Street Journal,* November 17, 1983, p. 1.

Uttal, Bro. "The Corporate Culture Vultures." *Fortune,* October 17, 1983, pp. 66–72.

Vancil, Richard F. "Better Management of Corporate Development." *Harvard Business Review* 50 (September-October 1972): 53–62.

———. *Decentralization: Managerial Ambiguity by Design.* Homewood, Ill.: Dow Jones–Irwin, 1979.

Vancil, Richard F., and Peter Lorange. "Strategic Planning in Diversified Companies." *Harvard Business Review* 53 (January-February 1975): 81–90.

Vroom, Victor H. *Work and Motivation.* New York: Wiley, 1964.

Walker, Jon E., and Curt Tausky. "An Analysis of Work Incentives." *Journal of Social Psychology* 116 (1982): 27–39.

"Wal-Mart: The Model Discounter." *Dun's Business Month* 120 (December 1982): 60.

Wanous, John P. *Organizational Entry: Recruitment, Selection and Socialization of Newcomers.* Reading, Mass.: Addison-Wesley, 1980.

Weber, Max. *The Theory of Social and Economic Organization.* Translated by A.M. Henderson and Talcott Parsons. New York: Free Press, 1947.

"What's Wrong with Management?" *Dun's Business Month* 119 (April 1982): 48.

"Why Book Publishers Are No Longer in Love with Romance Novels." *Business Week,* December 5, 1983, p. 157.

Wiegner, Kathleen K. "Back into the Race." *Forbes,* October 10, 1983, pp. 30–32.

——— "It's About Time." *Forbes,* April 25, 1983, pp. 41–42.

————. "The One That Almost Got Away." *Forbes,* January 31, 1983, pp. 46–47.

Wilensky, Harold. *Organizational Intelligence.* New York: Basic Books, 1967.

Williamson, Oliver E. *Corporate Control and Business Behavior: An Inquiry into the Effects of Organization Form on Enterprise Behavior.* Englewood Cliffs, N.J.: Prentice-Hall, 1970.

————. *Markets and Hierarchies: Analysis and Antitrust Implications.* New York: Free Press, 1975.

Wyckoff, Donald D., and W. Earl Sasser. *The Chain-Restaurant Industry.* Lexington, Mass.: Lexington Books, 1978.

INDEX